HELP!
I'M MARRIED!

*Marriage:
A Lifetime Experience*

THEODORE HUGHES

Copyright ©2020 Theodore Hughes

Published by Dust Jacket Press
Help! I'm Married! Marriage: A Lifetime Experience / Theodore Hughes

ISBN: 978-1-947671-89-8

All rights reserved. No portion of this publication may be reproduced, stored in a retrieval system, or transmitted in any form or by any means, except for brief quotations in printed reviews, without prior permission of Theodore Hughes. Requests may be submitted by email: theodorehughes@icloud.com.

Dust Jacket Press
P. O. Box 721243
Oklahoma City, OK 73172
www.dustjacket.com

All Scripture quotations not otherwise designated are from the King James Version of the Bible.

Permission to quote from the following additional copyrighted versions of the Bible is acknowledged with appreciation:

The Holy Bible, New International Version®, NIV®. Copyright ©1973, 1978, 1984, 2011 by Biblica, Inc.® Used by permission. All rights reserved worldwide.

New King James Version® (NKJV). Copyright © 1982 by Thomas Nelson. Used by permission. All rights reserved.

Holy Bible, New Living Translation (NLT), copyright © 1996, 2004, 2015 by Tyndale House Foundation. Used by permission of Tyndale House Publishers, Inc., Carol Stream, Illinois 60188. All rights reserved.

Dust Jacket logos are registered trademarks of Dust Jacket Press, Inc.

Cover & interior design: D. E. West / ZAQ Designs - Dust Jacket Creative Services
Icon credit: Freepik.com

Printed in the United States of America

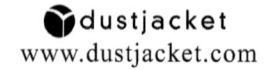

dustjacket
www.dustjacket.com

CONTENTS

Introduction v

1. Marriage Is God's Idea 1
2. Selecting a Spouse 23
3. Husband, Love Your Wife 33
4. Individuality vs. Individualism 43
5. Some Revelations Men Should Have About Women 53
6. Wife, Love Your Husband 65
7. Sexual Integrity Principles 77
8. Understanding the Purpose and Power of Men 117
9. General Scriptural Concepts Concerning Sexual Relations that Violate God's Sexual Principles and Consequences 121
10. The Power of a Woman's Influence 127
11. Personal Relationship Traits 137
12. Don't Tell on Me and I Won't Tell on You 149
13. The Voice of Marriage: Children 155
14. Love Must Be Full of Integrity 173
15. Unconditional Love Requires a Condition 187

16. Distractions 199

17. Jealousy 203

18. Integrity 213

19. A Digest of Marriage Concepts 221

20. Dialogue 241

21. Divorce 245

Bibliography 261
A Note from the Author 267

INTRODUCTION

Help! I'm Married!

I am very familiar with married couples who do not embrace Christ as the center focus of their marriage. As a matter of fact, I have friends who have not embraced Christ and are still faithful to each other after several years of being married. Yet I am still resolute that they are not living up to their marriage potential—that is, the possibility of a better marriage relationship.

It is true that a person's family history, temperament, coping skills, environment, and community contribute a great deal to the success or failure dynamics of a marriage relationship. However, the possibility of a more enhanced, meaningful, authentic, and true marriage awaits all who are willing to explore biblical principles as they relate to the marriage dynamic and incorporate them into their relationships.

Many times I have met with couples in which one partner does not believe in the existence of God or in the validity of the Holy Scriptures. This way of thinking places heavy tension in the room. Typically when a person is struggling and realizes that he or she needs help, the method used to help the person should not matter.

As I have explained on many occasions to those seeking marital counseling, the primary reason they're in my office in the first place is that something is broken in their relationship. My help centers around the incorporation of biblical principles. If one or both spouses resist this, I have to explain that there is no other sustainable foundation to build on to experience the fuller potential of a healthy marriage relationship. As I begin introducing individuals to biblical principles that have a direct bearing on specific issues in the marriage relationship, I enjoy seeing the change in people's countenances as the healing process is received and activated.

The unhealthy approach to the marriage relationship is the theory of automation. Automation is the technique of making an apparatus, a process, or a system operate without human intervention. Automation has its place in machines but is completely out of place when applied to human beings. Marriage is a non-retiring job that requires continuous practice and attention. Just as a person cannot take time off from breathing, so it is with marriage. For a relationship to stay online, we cannot go off-line. Two concepts need constant emphasis throughout the marriage relationship: (1) *It is not good that a man should be alone* and (2) *dwelling with a wife requires all knowledge.*

I remember that my mother always placed a decorative piece in the center of our kitchen table. Regardless who you looked at, the centerpiece was always in the line of sight. Mom could have easily removed it, but that would have taken away from its beautiful complement to the table. This meant that talking to someone included having the centerpiece as "part" of the conversation.

The same should be said of Christ. He must be at the *center* of all relationships, especially the marriage relationship. As couples engage in conversation of escalating stress (arguing), having Christ in view will always de-escalate the stress and change the outcome.

Having been involved in the gospel ministry for over forty-two years, I have not come across any married couple who said that they are hoping for a worthless and unfulfilled marriage relationship. Most married couples I have dealt with believe that marriage can be beautiful, sustainable, and fulfilling.

Once while watching a World Wrestling Federation match, I saw one wrestler pick up the referee and toss him out of the ring. With the absence of the referee, rules, courtesy, and common sense were replaced by anarchy. The self-declared winner was the wrestler who remained standing after the chaos.

The unmistakable observation about the person left standing was that he was officially alone. There was no referee to lift his arm as an official designation of victory, nor was there recognition by the World Wrestling Federation of his daring feat of rendering his opponent unconscious.

When biblical principles (rules or codes of conduct, standards for living) are not invited into the marriage relationship or if biblical principles are tossed out, chaos (a state of utter confusion) will occur. Also, significant emotional damage and possibly negative physical encounters will occur; certainly the marriage relationship will not reach its optimum potential.

Having conducted pre-marriage and post-wedding counseling for over forty-two years, I am convinced that having a difference-maker makes the difference. What do I mean? In many if not all the sports disciplines there is a referee (difference-maker), who is the keeper of the rules (rules of engagement). Without an absolute standard, each team can interject its own interpretation of the rules. If this kind of mind-set is adopted, the rules may even be suspended (temporarily or permanently).

Speaking along the lines of rules and standards, I have listened to individuals espouse the idea of being independent or free from restraints. If there were no social guidelines or "taboos" placed upon the marriage relationship, the experience would be so much better, they contend. Since logic is considered a consistency, this way of thinking is equal to doing away with all the rules governing driving a motor vehicle. Just imagine the disruptions, accidents, and hazards that would occur if such a position were universally accepted.

When we place intense thought to this type of thinking, we will discover that no standards or rules will become the standard or the rule. Considering this type of thinking must entail examination of motive and intent. The purpose of standards (in this case biblical standards) or rules is to insure harmony, balance, cohesiveness, and commitment to move a family, a community, a society of people forward with consideration for each of its members. Some circles suggest that a "higher power" or a "focus point" that is either tangible or intangible be called upon as the difference-maker in each relationship.

I once had the privilege of engaging in street evangelism in Darmstadt, Germany. I was told by a young man during a ministry encounter that he had determined that his higher power was a French fry. I do hope that he was just being combative; however, I responded by saying that when I got a bottle of ketchup he could say good-bye to his higher power. Because marriage stands out as a cornerstone of society, a person must be very careful in choosing a focus point or difference-maker, which must *not* be some abstract entity without self-sustainability.

I even noticed that some professional counselors are suggesting that couples go outside their marriage and build a relationship with someone else—while remaining married. This form of therapy goes against the fundamental principles of marriage vows that have their foundation in the Holy Scriptures. This type of relationship is called "open marriage," defined as a husband and wife who agree that they can have an intimate relationship with other people (male or female) without any retaliation or sting of conscience.

I'm reminded of a movie trailer for a film titled *Hall Pass*. When I was in grade school, students were not allowed to be in the hallway without supervision. The exception was being in the possession of a hall pass. If a student had to travel through the hallway, he or she would be given a hall pass, which gave him or her the authority to be out of the classroom without any fear of repercussion from a teacher, principal, or hall monitor. The movie *Hall Pass* emphasizes permission to engage in intimate relationship with someone other than a person's spouse. Even though this to some may sound good and feel good, I'm convinced that in the overall picture the end result will be *no* good.

Another type of relationship along this line is dubbed the "swingers" marriage, in which couples exchange mates with other couples for sex. Most swingers try to keep their swinging within a close-knit group. Avid swingers travel to clubs or groups with the intent of meeting married couples or singles who are willing to exchange partners for sex. Data suggests that some of these people do not have a sting of conscience from this activity because they do not get emotionally involved.

Some marriage therapists think that this contributes to a healthy marriage. To validate this kind of behavior, some couples say that their marriage relationship is so much better because they embrace the "open marriage" or "swingers" philosophy. This kind of relationship devalues and diminishes the concepts about the marriage relationship that are commonly held by society. Marriage is the sublime innate idea (a God factor) of two individuals, male and female, who purposely determine to go through life together to create family and community.

Every marriage has its moments of conflict. Thank about it: Two different people suddenly find themselves living in the same house with the intent of making it a home—only to discover that they are very different form each other. All their experiences, whether good or bad, move in with them. These experiences are called *baggage*. The potential for conflict is unavoidable.

Case in point: I know of a couple who had been married for a short time who decided to go on vacation. The wife was experienced in traveling by airplane. Her husband, however, had never traveled by airplane and thought it would be better to drive, which would deplete valued vacation time. The wife tried to convince her husband that traveling by air was very safe and that their vacation days would be longer at their destination. The coupled ended up flying, and the husband had a very stress-filled vacation because of the flight.

An unspoken thought threads its way through the marriage relationship—that the *other* person is responsible for making the marriage successful. The marriage vows are replete with principles of commitment, namely "love him/her, honor and keep him/her, in sickness and in health, *forsaking all others,* keep yourself only unto him/her so long as you both shall live."

A single person collecting and exchanging telephone numbers of friends carries the weight of relationship opportunities. Hence the memory becomes full of people contacts. When I asked a couple during a recent counseling session about their phone contacts, both had a substantial number. The woman had many male friend contacts and the gentleman had many female contacts. I asked, "How do you feel about your future wife [husband] having a contact list of other men [women]?" The collective response was "It's no problem. Our friends have our numbers too. I know her [his] friends and she [he] knows my friends."

I responded by saying, "Because marriage is exclusive—in that it centers around two people, male and female, committed to pushing forward through life together—I would like your individual response to the following scenario: One of you is taking a shower and the cell phone of the person in the shower rings. The time is midnight. The caller ID shows that it's a male [female]. A few minutes later the person steps out of the bathroom. Tell me—what would your response be having seen the caller ID?" Both parties said that the call would make them feel uncomfortable and decided that they would change their cell phone numbers to avoid this kind of controllable situation. However, some people consider it a "sport" to tamper with couples who are committed to the marriage relationship.

I am convinced that the devil does not want any couple to have a good marriage, let alone a great marriage. He will do anything necessary to present substitutes that will undermine and subsequently sabotage a marriage relationship. If you do not subscribe to this biblical fact, certainly you would at least recognize the constant threat coming from numerous sources against most marriages.

Genesis 1:26 states, "Then God said, 'Let us make man in our image, according to our likeness; let them have dominion over the fish of the sea, over the birds of the air, and over the cattle, over all the earth and over every creeping thing that creeps on the earth'" (NKJV).

According to Myles Monroe, the word *dominion* refers to a territory or sphere of influence or control; a territory of which a king or queen rules. The word *extrapolate*, according to Monroe, means to form an opinion or to make an estimate about something from known facts.

As we apply this understanding to God's marriage model, we see that He wants humanity to have rulership not only over animals but also over that which is earthly. Certainly anger, frustration, divorce, misunderstanding, domestic abuse, negative jealousy, dishonesty, pain, and so much more are of the earth.

Even though marriage is filled with uncertainties, doubt, and pressure, both internal and external, the possibility of a healthy marriage is still possible. Having a mind willing to embark on the road to a successful marriage is necessary. I think many married couples have surrendered their marital happiness, while remaining in or abandoning the relationship altogether, because of a sense of powerlessness to change what is happening right before their eyes. When a person retreats deep into his or her feelings or emotional center to become a silent sufferer, not realizing that Christ is the hope of glory, he or she will experience the stages of loss due to death, which are denial and isolation, anger, bargaining, depression, and finally acceptance. In many cases married couples create their own downward spiral with a push from our spiral enemy, Satan. The Scripture says that Jesus Christ was manifested to destroy all the works of Satan: "He that committeth sin is of the devil; for the devil sinneth from the beginning. For this purpose the Son of God was manifested, that he might destroy the works of the devil" (1 John 3:8).

The devil, also known as Satan or Lucifer, is an angel who deserted God's principles, idea, laws, and morals. This angel has a profound influence on marriage. We are dealing not just with the human dynamics but the spiritual aspects as well. As a biblical fact, Satan tried to usurp God's position in heaven. The proof texts to this fact are found in the verses below:

> *How art thou fallen from heaven, O Lucifer, son of the morning! how art thou cut down to the ground, which didst weaken the nations! For thou hast said in thine heart, I will ascend into heaven, I will exalt my throne above the stars of God: I will sit also upon the mount of the congregation, in the sides of the north: I will ascend above the heights of the clouds; I will be like the most High. Yet thou shalt be brought down to hell, to the sides of the pit.*
> (Isaiah 14:12–15)

> *You were in Eden,*
>   *the garden of God;*
> *every precious stone adorned you:*
>   *carnelian, chrysolite and emerald,*
>   *topaz, onyx and jasper,*
>   *lapis lazuli, turquoise and beryl.*
> *Your settings and mountings were made of gold;*
>   *on the day you were created they were prepared.*
> *You were anointed as a guardian cherub,*
>   *for so I ordained you.*
> *You were on the holy mount of God;*

> *you walked among the fiery stones.*
> *You were blameless in your ways*
>   *from the day you were created*
>   *till wickedness was found in you.*
> *Through your widespread trade*
>   *you were filled with violence,*
>   *and you sinned.*
> *So I drove you in disgrace from the mount of God,*
>   *and I expelled you, guardian cherub,*
>   *from among the fiery stones.*
> *Your heart became proud*
>   *on account of your beauty,*
> *and you corrupted your wisdom*
>   *because of your splendor.*
> *So I threw you to the earth;*
>   *I made a spectacle of you before kings.*
> *By your many sins and dishonest trade*
>   *you have desecrated your sanctuaries.*
> *So I made a fire come out from you,*
>   *and it consumed you,*
> *and I reduced you to ashes on the ground*
>   *in the sight of all who were watching.*
>
> (Ezekiel 28:13–18 NIV)

And he said unto them, I beheld Satan as lightning fall from heaven. Behold, I give unto you power to tread on serpents and scorpions, and over all the power of the enemy: and nothing shall by any means hurt you.

Notwithstanding in this rejoice not, that the spirits are subject unto you; but rather rejoice, because your names are written in heaven. In that hour Jesus rejoiced in spirit, and said, I thank thee, O Father, Lord of heaven and earth, that thou hast hid these things from the wise and prudent, and hast revealed them unto babes: even so, Father; for so it seemed good in thy sight.
(Luke 10:18–21)

God spared not the angels that sinned, but cast them down to hell, and delivered them into chains of darkness, to be reserved unto judgment.
(2 Peter 2:4)

And there was war in heaven: Michael and his angels fought against the dragon; and the dragon fought and his angels, and prevailed not; neither was their place found any more in heaven. And the great dragon was cast out, that old serpent, called the Devil, and Satan, which deceiveth the whole world: he was cast out into the earth, and his angels were cast out with him. And I heard a loud voice saying in heaven, Now is come salvation, and strength, and the kingdom of our God, and the power of his Christ: for the accuser of our brethren is cast down, which accused them before our God day and night.
(Revelation 12:7–10)

Even though there is a line of thought that denies the presence of an amoral entity in the world, the fact remains: there is a strong influence against moral discipline, and many marriages are either destroyed or deteriorate in some fashion, functioning below their potential or tolerated for various reasons.

I am persuaded that Satan, who is the god of this world, does not want marriage to be successful on any level. I am fully aware that some people do not believe that there is an evil presence in the world whose intent is to wreak havoc upon mankind. Irrespective of this concept of not believing in Satan's influence upon mankind, it is obvious that the marriage dynamic is severely challenged.

> *Thou believest that there is one God; thou doest well: the devils also believe, and tremble.*
> (James 2:1)

> *But if our gospel be hid, it is hid to them that are lost: in whom the god of this world hath blinded the minds of them which believe not, lest the light of the glorious gospel of Christ, who is the image of God, should shine unto them.*
> (2 Corinthians 4:3–4)

The devil will never reveal the result of a negative approach to a marital problem or issue. When an unhealthy resolution

...orsed by a married couple, it may seem good, feel good, and sound good. But when you examine the result of failed marriage relationships, you can clearly see from hindsight that the steps that led to the marriage destruction were not the right steps. Clyde M. Narramore wrote that time is the best counselor to determine whether something is right or wrong.

Wikipedia, a free online encyclopedia, states, "Marriage is a social union or legal contract between people called *spouses* that creates kinship. The definition of marriage varies according to different cultures, but usually an institution in which interpersonal relationships, usually intimate and sexual, are acknowledged."

Marriage is widely considered to be a state of being legally united to a person of the opposite sex in a consensual relationship. The concepts in this book will embrace the relational struggles of a marriage relationship. They will also help individuals contemplating marriage.

I'm convinced that a biblical relationship with God is necessary for a successful marriage. Everyone will need to talk to an outside party, either directly or indirectly, especially when the marriage relationship is shaky, sputtering, or stalled. These kinds of emotional challenges are a result of our human individuality and independence. Even if a friend, counselor, or minister is called upon, he or she can advise only up to a point. When biblical principles are embraced, the advice given will go further and more deeply because the Word of God never returns void and God will watch over His Word to assure its success. We should look at marriage difficulties not as closed doors but as a recipe for possibilities.

The Scriptures teach us that Christ is our high priest, who has endured stress, frustrations, difficulties, humiliations, rejections, persecutions, and so much more, from people and for people. Because of this, He has full knowledge of what we are feeling and can identify with our dilemmas. The higher power I recommend to be the difference-maker in the struggles of mankind, especially in the marriage relationship, is Jesus Christ, the Son of the living God.

> *For we have not an high priest which cannot be touched with the feeling of our infirmities; but was in all points tempted like as we are, yet without sin. Let us therefore come boldly unto the throne of grace, that we may obtain mercy, and find grace to help in time of need.*
> (Hebrews 4:15–16)

We've all heard the phrase "I know how you feel" countless times. The only one who really knows how you feel and what you're going through is our creator, God the Father, Son, and Holy Spirit. Too many married couples are living in a constant state of unnecessary tension.

When you think of it, life outside of the marriage relationship is full of negative challenges, uncertainties, and what are commonly known as half-truths. Validity, character, and integrity, when it comes to being genuine, are needed in marriage. The word *genuine* refers to what is sincerely and honestly felt and experienced.

Below are some of the emotional encounters of Jesus, the Son of God, which qualifies Him to help strengthen marriages.

1. Stress—a physical, chemical, or emotional factor that causes bodily or mental tension

> *An angel from heaven appeared to him and strengthened him. And being in anguish, he prayed more earnestly, and his sweat was like drops of blood falling to the ground. When he rose from prayer and went back to the disciples, he found them asleep, exhausted from sorrow.*
> (Luke 22:43–45 NIV)

Scientists have named the drops of blood coming from the sweat glands *hematidrosis,* which can happen when a person is under extreme stress.

Over my years of counseling couples, none of them have indicated to me that they were so stressful that drops of blood began oozing from their foreheads. Yet the tension, real or perceived, was very evident. There is a plethora of situations that can cause stress. The answer to these situations lies in our ability to process them using our internal filters.

By our *internal filters* I am referring to an individual's life history or, as is more commonly understood, his or her life story—that is, a person's ability to ping pong ideas, situations, or intense moments via his or her life experience to a satisfactory conclusion.

Stephen Covey in his book *The 7 Habits of Highly Effective People* states, "The word *paradigm* comes from the Greek. It was originally a scientific term and is more commonly used today to mean a mode, theory, perception, assumption, or frame of reference. In the more general sense, it's the way we 'see' the world—not in terms of our visual sense of sight but in terms of perceiving, understanding, and interpreting."

If individuals have a life story that is layered with unsuccessful conclusions, they may find it difficult to arrive at a successful resolution of a difficult moment. When a person awakens to an honest assessment of his or her weaknesses, that will be the platform or springboard from which he or she can get help. It's stated that "when your pain outweighs reluctance, then and only then you will seek help" (Pastor Terry Bates).

2. Frustration: a deep, chronic sense or state of insecurity and dissatisfaction arising from unresolved problems or unfulfilled needs

> *And I brought him to thy disciples, and they could not cure him. Then Jesus answered and said, O faithless and perverse generation, how long shall I be with you? how long shall I suffer you? bring him hither to me. And Jesus rebuked the devil; and he departed out of him: and the child was cured from that very hour.*
> (Matthew 17:16–18)

The problem with imperfection is imperfection. Imperfect people sometimes expect other individuals to be flawless. Apart from Jesus Christ, there has never been and never will be a perfect human being on earth. Yet a perfectionist mind-set exists among mankind. Two imperfect persons enter a marriage relationship, and one expects the other not to make mistakes or come up short in any certain area of his or her life.

Some marriages operate on a "prison system," in which one person is serving a life sentence while the other serves as warden. It is not hard to realize the unhealthy uneasiness of such a relationship. For a marriage relationship to be vibrant (pulsating with life), there must be the injection of balance and harmony.

The perfectionist mind-set can ignite frustration on many levels, such as the emotional, social, physical, spiritual, expectant, and so on. These can be real or perceived. In either case the frustration levels are the same.

3. Difficulties: controversy or disagreement

> *And one of them, named Caiaphas, being the high priest that same year, said unto them, Ye know nothing at all, nor consider that it is expedient for us, that one man should die for the people, and that the whole nation perish not. And this spake he not of himself: but being high priest that year, he prophesied that Jesus should die for that nation* (John 11:49–51)

The undeniable fact that we each have a history looms large. Our individual history contains a multiplicity of experiences. Every person has negative and positive experiences. These experiences will have an effect on the marriage relationship and will impact decisions and the direction of the marriage relationship. In many cases a person's personal history can be very conflictive as well.

4. Humiliation: reducing to a lower position in one's own eyes or others' eyes

> *They stripped him and put a scarlet robe on him, and then twisted together a crown of thorns and set it on his head. They put a staff in his right hand. Then they knelt in front of him and mocked him. "Hail, king of the Jews!" they said. They spit on him, and took the staff and struck him on the head again and again. After they had mocked him, they took off the robe and put his own clothes on him. Then they led him away to crucify him.*
> (Matthew 27:28–31 NIV)

Many individuals think that humility is weakness or demeaning. I would venture to say that the dichotomy (two cuts) of humility yields weakness on one side but strength on the other. Anyone can be a brute or bully. Sometimes the actions of a tyrant conceal insecurity. It takes a very strong and secure person to submit to getting under someone else to lift him or her up.

Humility in the marriage relationship is enlarged as each person looks down on the other simply to lift him or her up. Scripturally, Paul writing to the Roman church said, "We then that are strong ought to bear the infirmities of the weak and not to please ourselves" (Romans 15:1).

Every person comes with a set of weaknesses and strengths. In the marriage relationship the strength of the other person is there to support, help, defend, and cover the other person's weaknesses. This doesn't remove the responsibility to educate and warn a person of a weakness that will ultimately destroy the marriage. The idea is to avoid ridiculing a person for not measuring up to a certain standard rather than coming alongside the person during times of struggle.

I'm familiar with a situation wherein a husband reached out to his wife, placed his arms around her waist, and said, "Let me show you how much I love you." Afterward he proceeded to bite a hole into her lip. She screamed and pulled away as blood began gushing from her lip.

> *So after he had washed their feet, and had taken his garments, and was set down again, he said unto them, Know ye what I have done to you? Ye call me Master and Lord: and ye say well; for so I am. If I then, your Lord and Master, have washed your feet; ye also ought to wash one*

another's feet. For I have given you an example, that ye should do as I have done to you
(John 13:12–15)

Jesus did not just wash the disciples' feet just to get them to be nice to each other. His far greater goal was to extend his mission on earth after he was gone. These men were to move into the world serving God and serving all people as they presented the gospel message. With this divine principle being introduced into the marriage relationship, humility takes on a great meaning. Married men are not to demonstrate their physical powers over their wives but rather to demonstrate them to support and provide security for them.

5. Rejection: a refusal to accept or consider something or someone

He was in the world, and the world was made by him, and the world knew him not. He came unto his own, and his own received him not. (John 1:10–11)

Then Achish called David, and said unto him, Surely, as the Lord liveth, thou hast been upright, and thy going out and thy coming in with me in the host is good in my sight: for I have not found evil in thee since the day of thy coming unto me unto this day: nevertheless the lords favour thee not. Wherefore now return, and go in peace, that thou displease not the lords of the Philistines. And David said unto Achish, But what have I done? and what hast thou found in thy servant so long as I have been with thee unto this day, that I may not go fight against the enemies of my lord the king? And Achish answered and said to David, I know that thou art good in my sight, as an angel of God: notwithstanding the princes of the Philistines have said, He shall not go up with us to the battle. Wherefore now rise up early in the morning with thy master's servants that are come with thee: and as soon as ye be up early in the morning, and have light, depart. So David and his men rose up early to depart in the morning, to return into the land of the Philistines. And the Philistines went up to Jezreel. (1 Samuel 29:6–11)

And when Saul was come to Jerusalem, he assayed to join himself to the disciples: but they were all afraid of him, and believed not that he was a disciple. (Acts 9:26)

As in the life of Jesus, David and Paul experienced rejection. Regardless of how a person masks it, it is felt on the deepest emotional level. In short, rejection hurts and in some cases destroys a person's well-being, comfort, and security.

Many married couples are living in a constant state of rejection. It can range from simply refusing to hold a spouse's hand to refusing intimacy. Rejection can also be seen in several other actions, such as refusing to talk to the other spouse or going into another room and closing the door, which completes the wall of rejection. Tragically a spouse may mask rejection with various excuses to remain married. Being rejected while married is very unfair and cruel. Marriage should never be viewed as a lifelong prison sentence for one spouse while the other acts as the warden.

6. Persecution: harassing or punishing in a manner designed to injure, grieve, or afflict

> *All the people in the synagogue were furious when they heard this. They got up, drove him out of the town, and took him to the brow of the hill on which the town was built, in order to throw him off the cliff. But he walked right through the crowd and went on his way.*
> (Luke 4:28–30 NIV)

> *But they shouted, "Take him away! Take him away! Crucify him!"*
> *"Shall I crucify your king?" Pilate asked. "We have no king but Caesar," the chief priests answered. Finally Pilate handed him over to them to be crucified.* (John 19:15–16 NIV)

I remember a man in my neighborhood who treated his wife like one of his children. I was told that if she did not do something right, he would remove his belt and punish her with lashes. Being children and very curious, when this man's son told us how his father treated his mother, we could not understand how something like this could be possible. One evening his son reported that his parents were arguing and invited us to look through the window. To my surprise, the man was indeed beating her with a belt for an apparent infraction. I am convinced that there are many such harmful activities that take place behind closed doors and are ingeniously covered up in public

Scripture indicates another divine principle, that of the lifting-up of Christ. Because this is a divine principle, it doesn't matter the time, nature, or situation of when Christ is lifted up. He will cover the matter with all the elements necessary to resolve the issue.

I frequently use the illustration of tying objects to the opposite ends of a piece of string. After doing so, I lift the string from the center point. The two objects slowly come together, eventually touching again. This reminds me of a moment that my wife, Nadine, and I had a disagreement. When it was time to go to bed, I purposely perched myself at the very edge of the bed. I was determined not to touch her. This was absolutely ridiculous, of course.

Along this paradigm, I remember my mother and aunt yelling or using their outside voices between their two houses because they were some distance apart. In short, they yelled because they were not close. In marriage, couples yell back and forth also because they are not close—in a deeper sense. In marriage there must be alerts to signs of distance that occur in the small things and eventually the larger.

This principle is located in the verses below:

> *Jesus said, "This voice was for your benefit, not mine. Now is the time for judgment on this world; now the prince of this world will be driven out. And I, when I am lifted up from the earth, will draw all people to myself."*
> (John 12:30–32 NIV)

Whenever my wife and I are not on the same page, during my devotion time of prayer and praise to God, I am reminded to return to her and make the necessary apologies—and then return to God.

This principle is located in the following passage:

> *"Therefore if you bring your gift to the altar, and there remember that your brother has something against you, leave your gift there before the altar, and go your way. First be reconciled to your brother, and then come and offer your gift."*
> (Matthew 5:23–24 NKJV)

Many couples who would treat each other in a much more humane manner if they had the right information. I frequently encourage married couples and those contemplating marriage to read books concerning marriage and relationship.

There is an unspoken understanding that says, "You are a woman and I am a man. What more do we need?" Anything of worth and value needs to be studied, examined, and contemplated to extract the best concepts possible for it to continue.

Bookstores and many libraries are full of great reading material on marriage and relationships. Marriage is so complicated that a thorough and ongoing knowledge of this subject must take place throughout a couple's married life.

The principle for this concept is found in this passage from Hosea:

> *My people are destroyed for lack of knowledge: because thou hast rejected knowledge, I will also reject thee, that thou shalt be no priest to me: seeing thou hast forgotten the law of thy God, I will also forget thy children.* (Hosea 4:6)

Some people *invest* in joint or separate vacations, hoping that they will find that missing element that made their marriage worthwhile. Many individuals invest in cars, jewelry, exercise programs, reciting their marriage vows, and counseling, trying to regain that *elusive something* that would convince them that the time and effort required in developing or continuing a meaningful marriage relationship is worth their *time* and *energy*.

I am fully aware that the tragedy of broken marriage relationships can become so severe that the parties end up in divorce proceedings. It has been my observation that individuals entering a marriage relationship do so with *longevity* in mind or, as the marriage vows say, "until death do us part."

The "until death do us part" principle is illustrated in the book of Ruth. Ruth was a Moabite with a remarkably different belief system from that of the Israelites. Ruth's husband had died and her mother-in-law, Naomi, had determined to return to Bethlehem because of news that the famine had ended and that God was supplying food for His people. Naomi told Ruth to return to her people and her gods. But Ruth was equally determined to travel back to Bethlehem with Naomi.

But Ruth said,

> *"Entreat me not to leave you,*
> *Or to turn back from following after you;*
> *For wherever you go, I will go;*
> *And wherever you lodge, I will lodge;*
> *Your people shall be my people,*
> *And your God, my God.*
> *Where you die, I will die,*
> *And there will I be buried.*
> *The Lord do so to me, and more also,*
> *If anything but death parts you and me."*
> (Ruth 1:16–17 NKJV)

Happily ever after is not a fairy tale. It's a choice.
—Fawn Weaver

George Barna's statistical studies revealed, "There no longer seems to be much of a stigma attached to divorce; it is now seen as an unavoidable rite of passage. . . . Interviews with young adults suggest that they want their initial marriage to last but are not particularly optimistic about that possibility."

There is evidence that many young people are moving toward embracing the idea of a "serial marriage," in which a person gets married two or three times, seeking a different partner for each phase of his or her adult life: young adult, mid-adult, and older adult.

During my track and field days at Violet Consolidated and Saint Bernard High School, the track team's exercise regimen included circling the track at least one time at full stride. Starting out was almost entertaining, to say the least. Passing through the first turn and the second after a short but curved turn posed no great energy drain. Heading down the back straightaway, however, convinced us that we were expending energy out of which we became concerned about our stamina to reach the finish line. The third turn was the most dreaded, because fatigue was becoming more pronounced. When we would enter and exit the fourth turn, our legs were hard to propel forward—everything in us said to stop running. But our coach said, "When you hit the wall, just keep running. You'll get your second wind and reach the finish line."

All marriages will "hit the wall" at some point. This sometimes-unexpected wall can surface multiple times during a lengthy marriage relationship. What you do and how you conduct yourself at this moment will determine how your marriage is punctuated. I am convinced that Christ is the difference-maker.

Marriage is not a pain-free journey. As a matter of fact, marriage is filled with painful moments.

Painful moments in marriage can be so disruptive that tears turn into anger and anger turns into action—and the action can be either positive or negative. It can be positive in that the person will use focused energy to fix or address the problem with understanding and humility.

I discovered that individuals enter into marriage with high ideals—only to discover how dissimilar they are from their spouses.

If marriage had no challenges, there would be no divorces. *The greatest challenge in marriage is remembering that your spouse is not perfect.* The destructive vice is the conscious demand of perfection from one's spouse. My observation and personal experience have brought me to this conclusion: a spouse will never be what the other person has mentally imagined him or her to be.

Living up to another person's expectations without the possibility of failure is very difficult. Many people are comfortable with their own failures but are very irritated at someone else's shortcomings.

Our mental images change constantly.

Trying to live up to an imperfect person's expectations places stress on the person demanding and the person being demanded. I'm not saying that spouses should abrogate their responsibility to engage each other on issues that threaten the marriage relationship but rather that they should be in touch with self-development, compassion, and understanding toward each other. For example, your spouse may not be strong in the area of housekeeping. Instead of creating hostility about it, go ahead and clean the house yourself and enjoy the evening.

Clean the house yourself
and enjoy the evening.

I think that spousal difference has merit with regard to balance and supportive benefit. The revealer of our dissimilarity with regard to dealing with the challenges of life is *time*. Let me go on record by saying that there is nothing wrong with anticipating the best practicality in a marriage.

If it were not for the marriage dream, the dreamers would never marry. But the hot truth is that *the greatest earthly barrier to the fulfillment of the marriage dream is the individual.*

If marriage is a dream, then don't wake up.

The principles presented in this book can transform your marriage into a dynamic, romantic, and others-centered representation of the heart of God.

Don't turn your rose into a thornbush (Nadine A. Hughes).

1

Marriage Is God's Idea

All of God's creation has within itself the seed for the continuation of its species or fruit. If God were not forward thinking, self-contained existence would stop at its first creation. Genesis records that fruit, animals, and mankind have their future within themselves.

> *And God said, Let the earth bring forth grass, the herb yielding seed, and the fruit tree yielding fruit after his kind, whose seed is in itself, upon the earth: and it was so.* (Genesis 1:11)

> *And God created great whales, and every living creature that moveth, which the waters brought forth abundantly, after their kind, and every winged fowl after his kind: and God saw that it was good.* (Genesis 1:21)

> *And God said, Let the earth bring forth the living creature after his kind, cattle, and creeping thing, and beast of the earth after his kind: and it was so. And God made the beast of the earth after his kind, and cattle after their kind, and every thing that creepeth upon the earth after his kind: and God saw that it was good.* (Genesis 1:24–25)

God saw from an eternal perspective. He looked into the eternal present, past and future, with consideration of what he had just created. God determined from all vantage points—philosophically, socially, theoretically, and actually—that what He had created was eternally good.

This eternal perspective included both male and female, who possess the image of almighty God. Below are absolute principles that stand out in the marriage relationship.

> *So God created man in his own image, in the image of God created he him; male and female created he them.* (Genesis 1:27)

Scripture is very clear about the characteristics of God, who is a Spirit.

> *God is a Spirit: and they that worship him must worship him in spirit and in truth.* (John 4:24)

Now the Lord is that Spirit: and where the Spirit of the Lord is, there is liberty.
(2 Corinthians 3:17)

Now unto the King eternal, immortal, invisible, the only wise God, be honour and glory for ever and ever. Amen. (1 Timothy 1:17)

For since the creation of the world His invisible attributes are clearly seen, being understood by the things that are made, even His eternal power and Godhead, so that they are without excuse. (Romans 1:20 NKJV)

For by Him all things were created that are in heaven and that are on earth, visible and invisible, whether thrones or dominions or principalities or powers. All things were created through Him and for Him. And He is before all things, and in Him all things consist. (Colossians 1:16–17 NKJV)

Since God is a Spirit and obviously invisible, it is reasonable to state that the characteristics of God are intangible, not of physical substance.

The Scriptures refer to God in human terms but don't change the fact that God is a Spirit. He is infinite, eternal, and unchangeable in His being, wisdom, power, holiness, justice, goodness, and truth, in which all things have their beginning, support, and end. Below are scriptures that attribute human characteristics to God.

A. God's hand

And I will stretch out my hand, and smite Egypt with all my wonders which I will do in the midst thereof: and after that he will let you go. (Exodus 3:20)

B. God's arm

Wherefore say unto the children of Israel, I am the Lord, and I will bring you out from under the burdens of the Egyptians, and I will rid you out of their bondage, and I will redeem you with a stretched out arm, and with great judgments. (Exodus 6:6)

C. God's ear

Incline thine ear, O Lord, and hear; open thine eyes, O Lord, and see: and hear all the words of Sennacherib, which hath sent to reproach the living God.
(Isaiah 37:17)

D. God's foot

Thus saith the Lord, The heaven is my throne, and the earth is my footstool: where is the house that ye build unto me? and where is the place of my rest?
(Isaiah 66:1)

E. God's coming and going

Oh that thou wouldest rend the heavens, that thou wouldest come down, that the mountains might flow down at thy presence, as when the melting fire burneth, the fire causeth the waters to boil, to make thy name known to thine adversaries, that the nations may tremble at thy presence! (Isaiah 64:1–2)

The eyes of the Lord run to and fro throughout the whole earth, to shew himself strong in the behalf of them whose heart is perfect toward him. (2 Chronicles 16:9)

It is obvious that these references to bodily members are to be understood metaphorically or as a figure of speech, in which a word or phrase is used in place of another to suggest a likeness. God does not have to have a human body to create a human body. For example, just because I plant tomatoes and cabbage doesn't make me a vegetable.

Image is a reproduction of a person or object. We can see in Scripture that males as well as females were created in the image of God. The Hebrew definition of *image* is "resemblance." The image of God is the intangible qualities of mankind.

These invisible qualities give mankind the capacity to have healthy and enduring relationships, especially the marriage relationship. The image of God in mankind cannot be weighed on a scale or measured with a ruler. The image of God is visible when it is demonstrated and received.

Below are several examples of the characteristics of the image of God in mankind and subsequent Scripture references.

A. Love

In all their affliction he was afflicted, and the angel of his presence saved them: in his love and in his pity he redeemed them; and he bare them, and carried them all the days of old. (Isaiah 63:9)

Greater love hath no man than this, that a man lay down his life for his friends. (John 15:13)

And hope maketh not ashamed; because the love of God is shed abroad in our hearts. (Romans 5:5)

B. Compassion
   1. Kindness: the quality of being friendly or considerate
   2. Sympathy: the feeling of pity and sorrow for someone else's troubles
   3. Empathy: the ability to understand and share the feelings of another
   4. Tenderness: showing gentleness to someone else
   5. Longsuffering: having or showing patience in spite of troubles
   6. Feeling: a reaction to or from something
   7. Truth: that which is true or in accordance with facts or reality
   8. Honesty: freedom from deceit; sincerity

C. **Peace**

Thou wilt keep him in perfect peace, whose mind is stayed on thee: because he trusteth in thee. (Isaiah 26:3)

Great peace have they which love thy law: and nothing shall offend them. (Psalm 119:165)

Peace I leave with you, my peace I give unto you: not as the world giveth, give I unto you. Let not your heart be troubled, neither let it be afraid. (John 14:27)

Finally, brethren, farewell. Be perfect, be of good comfort, be of one mind, live in peace; and the God of love and peace shall be with you. (2 Corinthians 13:11)

1. Trust: the firm belief in the reliability or strength of someone or something
2. Safety: the condition of being protected from danger, risk, or injury
3. Freedom: the power to act, speak, or think without restraint
4. Justice: being fair and reasonable; just treatment
5. Mercy: compassion toward someone whom it is in one's power to punish or harm
6. Balance: an even distribution; remaining upright and steady

7. Temperance: restraining oneself form indulging in something
8. Calm: not showing anger or strong or intense feelings
9. Tolerance: sympathy or indulgence for opinions or behavior that one does not agree with.

D. Joy

Therefore with joy shall ye draw water out of the wells of salvation. (Isaiah 12:3)

Therefore the redeemed of the Lord shall return, and come with singing unto Zion; and everlasting joy shall be upon their head: they shall obtain gladness and joy; and sorrow and mourning shall flee away. (Isaiah 51:11)

For your shame ye shall have double; and for confusion they shall rejoice in their portion: therefore in their land they shall possess the double: everlasting joy shall be unto them. (Isaiah 61:7)

These things have I spoken unto you, that my joy might remain in you, and that your joy might be full. (John 15:11)

For the kingdom of God is not meat and drink; but righteousness, and peace, and joy in the Holy Ghost. (Romans 14:17)

1. Happiness: feeling or showing pleasure or contentment
2. Assurance: a positive declaration intended to give confidence; a promise
3. Hope: a feeling of expectation and desire for a certain thing to happen
4. Anticipation: a prediction
5. Expectation: a strong belief that something will happen
6. Satisfaction: fulfillment of one's wishes or needs
7. Contentment: happiness with one's situation in life
8. Zeal: great energy in pursuit of an objective
9. Approval: the action of officially agreeing to something or belief that someone is acceptable.

E. **Faithfulness**
   1. Dependability: trustworthiness and reliability
   2. Choice: an act of selecting when faced with two or more possibilities
   3. Camaraderie: mutual trust and friendship among people who spend a lot of time together
   4. Friendship: a bond of mutual affection between people
   5. Strength: quality or state of being physically strong; influence or power possessed by a person, organization, or country

6. *United: joined together for a common purpose or feeling*
7. *Agreement: harmony in opinion or feeling*
8. *Knowledge: facts, information, and skills acquired by a person through experience or education*
9. *Insightfulness: having or showing an accurate and deep understanding.*

The human body is the vehicle for the visible expression of the image of God. This can be understood more clearly in the scriptures below:

> *In the beginning was the Word, and the Word was with God, and the Word was God. The same was in the beginning with God.*
> (John 1:1–2)

> *And the Word was made flesh, and dwelt among us, (and we beheld his glory, the glory as of the only begotten of the Father,) full of grace and truth.* (John 1:14)

> *And God blessed them, and God said unto them, Be fruitful, and multiply, and replenish the earth, and subdue it: and have dominion over the fish of the sea, and over the fowl of the air, and over every living thing that moveth upon the earth.* (Genesis 1:28)

It's amazing how much trust God must have in mankind. He has given dominion of the entire earth to His crowning creation. Thank about it—everything that pertains to earth, that which is under the sun, is to be controlled by mankind. That's precisely why mankind needs to be under the direction of God, for if mankind is out of control, what he *controls* will be out of control.

The word *mystery* is something that is either difficult or impossible to understand. From the intelligent design perspective, creation is not a mystery to be solved but rather a mystery to be *lived*. The above record gives insight into the origins of all things.

Included in the origins of various animals and plants is the origin of the nan and the woman. As a matter of fact, creation is God's idea. Creation is a choice and an expression of God's love.

Creation of man

> *And the Lord God formed man of the dust of the ground, and breathed into his nostrils the breath of life; and man became a living being.*
> (Genesis 2:7 NKJV)

"Dust of the ground" implies that there is nothing fancy about the chemical elements making up our bodies. The body is a lifeless shell until God brings it alive with his "breath of life."

> *Then the Lord God took the man and put him in the garden of Eden to tend and keep it.*
> (Genesis 2:15 NKJV)

God gave Adam the *responsibility* of taking care of the garden, which was in Eden. This job was given to Adam before he was married. It is amazing how many couples commit themselves to marriage without a commitment to a job. I typically ask the man during premarital counseling sessions if he has a job. If the response is no, I begin a new line of counseling.

I am constantly amazed at the action plan of engaged couples when asked, "Where are you going to live when you get married?" Again these responses come from individuals who want to get married but have not yet secured employment. Some say that they'll live with one of their parents. One lady said that she would live with her parents and he would live with his. I'm even aware of couples who moved in with friends who were also married.

> *And the Lord God commanded the man, saying, Of every tree of the garden thou mayest freely eat: But of the tree of the knowledge of good and evil, thou shalt not eat of it: for in the day that thou eatest thereof thou shalt surely die. And the Lord God said, It is not good that the man should be alone; I will make him an help meet for him.*
> (Genesis 2:16–18)

In part of the passage above, God is having a face-to-face conversation with Adam. This is known as a *dialogue*, which is customarily between two individuals. God is telling Adam that even though he is here with him, he (Adam) is alone. Another perspective is that God is saying, "I am different from you. The animals are different from you, and the plants are different from you. You really need someone who is like you."

This is a principle that is often overlooked or ignored. "It is not good that the man should be alone" (Genesis 2:18). Men in many cases are self-talkers. A man can have a complete conversation with his wife or girlfriend without her actually being present.

Here is a real-life example of how this scenario plays out. The man is sitting on the sofa hoping that his wife will come and sit next to him. He waits a while, and finally his wife begins heading in his direction. In his mind he begins to get excited. Instead of sitting next to him, however, she moves to her next task. Then the man says to himself, "Forget it." This drama takes place in a man's mind and his wife is totally clueless. I surmise from mentoring men that quite a few have deep conversations with their wives in their minds. In many cases when the husband arrives home he has nothing much to say to his wife because he is exhausted from having "talked" with her throughout the day.

As men we need to learn to be better communicators. Society presses men to think that only women communicate their inner thoughts and emotional pain readily. Men are not pain free or emotionally numb. The well-known statement "No man is an island" has a very practical application. Men in particular need to be very careful about trying to go it alone. Below are some proof-text scriptures to validate this point.

A National Geographic program I once watched featured a segment showing a male lion lying under a tree on a hill. Then the camera panned to lionesses and lion cubs interacting, climbing over the lionesses, play-fighting with each other, and at times receiving nourishment.

With this entire activity just yards away, the male lion remains alone. In most cases he is actively on guard to protect his pride from attack and the usurping of his dominance over his lioness and clubs. Periodically he would roar, serving to alert any opposition as to his presence and his willingness to protect his territory and family.

Yet the picture is still profound about the isolation that many men find themselves in with no apparent plan to resolve this position. Many will flex their manhood so as to convince those nearby of their dominance but lack of interdependence. "It is not good that the man should be alone." When men and women understand this principle, their marriage relationship will be healthier and productive if they take the necessary steps to offset this isolation.

Here are some excuses men use to justify being isolated:

1. I need to get away before I do something that I would regret.
2. I need to clear my head.

3. I am under a lot of stress.
4. I am tired of hearing my wife's point of view.
5. I am doing the best I can—I don't want to be bothered.
6. I don't know.
7. I don't care.
8. I don't want to disappoint.
9. I have made silence a friend.
10. I cannot finish a complete thought.
11. I talk but I am not heard.

> *There is one alone, and there is not a second; yea, he hath neither child nor brother: yet is there no end of all his labour; neither is his eye satisfied with riches; neither saith he, For whom do I labour, and bereave my soul of good? This is also vanity, yea, it is a sore travail. Two are better than one; because they have a good reward for their labour. For if they fall, the one will lift up his fellow: but woe to him that is alone when he falleth; for he hath not another to help him up. Again, if two lie together, then they have heat: but how can one be warm alone? And if one prevail against him, two shall withstand him; and a threefold cord is not quickly broken.*
> (Ecclesiastes 4:8–12)

> *And the Lord God caused a deep sleep to fall upon Adam and he slept: and he took one of his ribs, and closed up the flesh instead thereof.* (Genesis 2:21)

Just because God removed a rib from Adam does not mean that men are born with one less rib. If a man has an amputated leg, it doesn't mean that each of his children will be born with a missing leg.

> *And the rib, which the Lord God had taken from man, made he a woman, and brought her unto the man. And Adam said, This is now bone of my bones, and flesh of my flesh: she shall be called Woman, because she was taken out of Man.* (Genesis 2:22–23)

God could have made the woman from the dust of the ground, as he made man. God chose, however to create the woman from Adam's bone. In so doing, God illustrated for us that in marriage the man and woman symbolically become one flesh. Throughout the scriptures God treats marriage seriously.

When someone thinks deeply about the creation process from a human perspective, he or she discovers that man gives life to the woman and the woman gives life to the world. There is therefore is no room for one gender to feel superior or less superior to the other because each carries exclusive advantages.

Adam accepted Eve and recognized that she was the fulfillment of his current need for companionship and future happiness.

Restaurants that serve barbeque ribs usually have different kinds of sauces on the table that can be applied to the portion of ribs ordered. Now it is not mandatory to use these sauces or even salt or pepper. Yet the sauce in most cases enhances the rib-eating experience. During marriage counseling I use this analogy to drive home the point to men about complementing their wives in various ways in order to bring out their best "flavors."

God gave marriage as a gift to Adam and Eve. They were a marriage made under the careful engineering of God the Father, Son, and Holy Spirit. Marriage was not brought about by culture or just for convenience. It was instated by God and has four basic aspects:

1. God has to be invited into the process.
2. The man leaves his parents and promises himself to his wife.
3. The man and woman are joined together by taking responsibility for each other's well-being.
4. The two become one flesh through the intimacy of sexual union.

Adam's acceptance of a spouse was very narrowed and focused. In short, Eve was Adam's first and only choice of a spouse. This gives new meaning to the commonly used phrase

"She is the one." Scripture gives us some healthy guidelines for selecting or choosing a spouse. God gave Adam and Eve bodies in order to be able to express the image of God in them in a tangible way. Look again at Genesis 2:23—

> *And Adam said, This is now bone of my bones, and flesh of my flesh: she shall be called Woman, because she was taken out of Man.*

The woman was taken out of the man; that is, when God made the woman, he removed one of Adam's ribs and made the woman. This indicates that the woman had all the dynamics of Adam—and a little bit more.

Adam was a complete entity, unique and a fully functional human being. When God created Eve, she was all of Adam and a little bit more. Eve had the capacity to give birth to another human being, a highly active sensitivity, compassion, tolerance, gentleness, empathy, the ability to nurture a child, and so much more. Eve was created in such a way that she deserved a high level of respect, protection, and support from Adam.

This is the break point where men and women have their greatest dilemmas. A man can have a conversation with another man and for the most part they relate. The dialogue may or may not contain lengthy sentences. Yet the law of communication works smoothly and in many cases seamlessly. The same can be said of woman-to-woman communication. The communication difficulty that exists between men and women is echoed in phrases such as "Why can't you understand?" "He just doesn't get it." "You're not making any sense." 'Why are you crying?" "I need to take a ride." "I'm going to my mother's house." "You never understand me." "Why can you not listen?" "Could you be quiet for a moment?" "I'm done." "Why does it have to be *your* way all the time?"

The failure in communication doesn't rest in not knowing or wanting to know the other person's language. When the bridge that leads to dialogue has been built through language-learning tutorials, then communication can flow. Then being understood and understanding will strengthen the marriage relationship.

The communication dynamic between married couples is not that either possesses greater capacity then the other. The dynamic is that male and female are created in the image of God with differences. Adam in the creation story was Adam, who came from the dirt, and Eve came out of the dirt as well. There must be an appreciation for the image of God in both male and female that is evident.

There must also be an appreciation for the contribution that both spouses bring to the marriage relationship. There must also be a sincere and an ongoing effort to understand the other person's language. This is a bridge and not a barrier to good, wholesome communication. I remember when my mother, Josephine Hughes, and my aunt, Verna Mae Payne, lived a few houses apart. As noted earlier, they would yell back and forth hoping that they were getting their message across.

They yelled because they were not close to each other and did not have telephones.

The concept is still true today. Spouses are in the same house, sleep in the same bed, and sit together—but are not close. The result is yelling. Couples who argue unfairly remind me of a tennis match. Each person is just waiting to see the direction or travel of the ball after the single intent, to hit the ball. Putting one's racquet down and closing the distance or separation is an act of seeking the greater good for the relationship.

Adam and Eve were created fully grown with the capacity to reproduce after their kind. God created sexual intimacy. He endowed Adam and Eve with the capacity to have children and the desire to enjoy the pleasure of sexual relationship with each other within the context of marriage.

> *Therefore a man shall leave his father and mother and be joined to his wife, and they shall become one flesh.* (Genesis 2:24 NKJV)

Leave simply means to go away from a person, object, or location. For some misguided reason some couples I have counseled have attempted to reinvent the meaning of this common word. Although I'm sure there are some legitimate reasons, here are some questionable justifications I have heard for living with parents while married: "It's just for a little while," "We're doing it until we get enough money," "We'll stay with them until we get jobs," "We're staying with them while we're still in school," "My parents have a big house."

In the words of Fawn Weaver, "You don't marry one person—you marry three: the person you think they are, the person they are, and the person they're going to become as a result of being married to you."

Home is where your greatest treasury lives.

Adam immediately realized that his wife occupied a very special place in his life that went beyond the close relationship of parents. God never wanted children to disavow their parents but rather to understand the relationship dynamics of a husband and a wife. All things being equal, parents generally prepare, by way of example, their children to interact with society and its various levels of relationships, in particular the marriage relationship.

> *And they were both naked, the man and his wife, and were not ashamed.*
> (Genesis 2:25 NKJV)

The Hebrew word for *ashamed* in this verse means "to be disappointed or to be delayed." A common meaning of the word deals with feeling disgraced or inferior.

With the above definition in mind, let me share something that happened to me and my brother, Walter, a few days before Christmas when we were boys. My mother had purchased two bicycles; one was for Walter and the other for me. We saw the boxes they were in before Christmas and wanted to ride them so badly that we pestered my mother, even with tears, to allow us to ride our Christmas gifts.

My mother explained that it was not right to ride our bikes before Christmas. Because of our relentlessness, though, our mother finally gave the go-ahead. Walter and I pulled our bikes out of their containers and off we went.

We were enjoying the ride until the unthinkable happened. My brother's foot pedal and my front tire merged. Some of the tire spokes of my front tire were ripped while others were bent, causing the rim to bend out of shape. Needless to say, I was saddened considerably—and wished that I had not enjoyed my Christmas gift days before Christmas. When Christmas Day arrived, the normal joy or excitement of a first-time experience was gone.

Similar to this, I counsel engaged couples not to enter into sexual relationship until they are married. To couples who are already cohabitating, I ask them to abstain from sexual relations until they are married. After making this directive, I place the policing of this matter to the conscience and integrity of the couples themselves. I will talk extensively about sexual integrity in a later chapter of this book.

"Passionate sex is great. A passionate marriage filled with passionate sex is so much better" (Fawn Weaver).

2

Selecting a Spouse

Presenting a proposal to marry and accepting a proposal to marry are very serious matters. As a matter of fact, many ministers' manuals state, "Marriage is to be entered into advisedly, reverently, and soberly." Some of the non-biblical guidelines for selecting a spouse are as follows:

1. Live together to ensure compatibility.
2. Date as many people as possible before making a final selection.
3. Select the most beautiful girl possible.
4. Select the most handsome man possible.
5. Select someone who has lots of money.
6. Select someone who is famous.
7. Select someone who is popular.
8. Select someone who makes you happy.
9. Let someone else select your potential spouse.
10. Select someone whom you like to have sex with.

11. Select someone whom your parents would like.
12. Select someone to get you out of your parents' home and authority.
13. Marry only someone of your own kind.

The Holy Scriptures reveal that social biases and stereotypes existed not as a declaration from heaven but as a preference among people. This kind of social preference, which divides people, was addressed long before activists raised their voices as indicated in the scriptures that follow.

> *And Adam called his wife's name Eve; because she was the mother of all living.* (Genesis 3:20)

An ancient Hebrew custom states that if you name someone, you control, provide, protect, house, nurture, teach, lead, and love him or her.

> *Then saith the woman of Samaria unto him, How is it that thou, being a Jew, askest drink of me, which am a woman of Samaria? for the Jews have no dealings with the Samaritans.*
> (John 4:9)

> *And as Peter was coming in, Cornelius met him, and fell down at his feet, and worshipped him. But Peter took him up, saying, Stand up; I myself also am a man. And as he talked with*

him, he went in, and found many that were come together. And he said unto them, Ye know how that it is an unlawful thing for a man that is a Jew to keep company, or come unto one of another nation; but God hath shewed me that I should not call any man common or unclean. (Acts 10:25–28)

Then Peter opened his mouth, and said, Of a truth I perceive that God is no respecter of persons: But in every nation he that feareth him, and worketh righteousness, is accepted with him. (Acts 10:34–35)

For as I passed by, and beheld your devotions, I found an altar with this inscription, To The Unknown God. Whom therefore ye ignorantly worship, him declare I unto you. God that made the world and all things therein, seeing that he is Lord of heaven and earth, dwelleth not in temples made with hands; Neither is worshipped with men's hands, as though he needed any thing, seeing he giveth to all life, and breath, and all things; And hath made of one blood all nations of men for to dwell on all the face of the earth, and hath determined the times before appointed, and the bounds of their habitation;

> *That they should seek the Lord, if haply they might feel after him, and find him, though he be not far from every one of us: For in him we live, and move, and have our being; as certain also of your own poets have said, For we are also his offspring.* (Acts 17:23–28)

Every animal and every plant was created to produce after its "kind." So it is with male and female, regardless of culture, ethnos, religion, or geographical region. If a man and woman marry, they have the ability to produce after their kind, that being another human being.

Yet the Scriptures indicate that God has given mankind the ability to choose. If this were not so, God would not have set before us more than one position as seen in His Word. The word *automation* is "the technique of making an apparatus, a process, or a system operate involuntarily or unconsciously." A machine, all things being equal, functions. Yet that same machine does not do so based on self-will. If it is cold, it doesn't ask for a blanket; it is hot it doesn't ask for a glass of water; if is tired it doesn't ask for time off or put in for a vacation. A machine does only what it is programed and maintained to do.

There is *more appreciation* for an effort given when it is done so from the personal will. When a person does something from an act of will, that action conveys to the receptive side of an individual that a thought process took place. A machine has no personalized thought processes. It simply does what it has been built or programed to do. At no time does God want mankind to be disengaged from their ability to willingly engage in an activity as seen in the verses below:

> *And the servant said unto him, Peradventure the woman will not be willing to follow me unto this land: must I needs bring thy son again unto the land from whence thou camest? And Abraham said unto him, Beware thou that thou bring not my son thither again.*
> (Genesis 24:5–6)

> *And they came, every one whose heart stirred him up, and every one whom his spirit made willing, and they brought the Lord's offering to the work of the tabernacle of the congregation, and for all his service, and for the holy garments.*
> (Exodus 35:21)

> *The gold for things of gold, and the silver for things of silver, and for all manner of work to be made by the hands of artificers. And who then is willing to consecrate his service this day unto the Lord? Then the chief of the fathers and princes of the tribes of Israel and the captains of thousands and of hundreds, with the rulers of the king's work, offered willingly.*
> (1 Chronicles 29:5–6)

I know also, my God, that thou triest the heart, and hast pleasure in uprightness. As for me, in the uprightness of mine heart I have willingly offered all these things: and now have I seen with joy thy people, which are present here, to offer willingly unto thee.
(1 Chronicles 29:17)

But without thy mind would I do nothing; that thy benefit should not be as it were of necessity, but willingly. (Philemon 14)

For if there be first a willing mind, it is accepted according to that a man hath, and not according to that he hath not.
(2 Corinthians 8:12)

For if I do this thing willingly, I have a reward: but if against my will, a dispensation of the gospel is committed unto me.
(1 Corinthians 9:17)

Feed the flock of God which is among you, taking the oversight thereof, not by constraint, but willingly; not for filthy lucre, but of a ready mind. (1 Peter 5:2)

The Lord is not slack concerning his promise, as some men count slackness; but is longsuffering to

> *us-ward, not willing that any should perish, but that all should come to repentance.*
> (2 Peter 3:9)

> *And Ruth said, Intreat me not to leave thee, or to return from following after thee: for whither thou goest, I will go; and where thou lodgest, I will lodge: thy people shall be my people, and thy God my God: Where thou diest, will I die, and there will I be buried: the Lord do so to me, and more also, if ought but death part thee and me.*
> (Ruth 1:16–17)

God has given mankind the ability to use their will to consider known facts and subsequently provide an opportunity to decide between two or more courses of action.

> *And the Lord God commanded the man, saying, Of every tree of the garden thou mayest freely eat: But of the tree of the knowledge of good and evil, thou shalt not eat of it: for in the day that thou eatest thereof thou shalt surely die.*
> (Genesis 2:16–17)

> *I call heaven and earth to record this day against you, that I have set before you life and death, blessing and cursing: therefore choose life, that both thou and thy seed may live.*
> (Deuteronomy 30:19)

And Elijah came unto all the people, and said, How long halt ye between two opinions? if the Lord be God, follow him: but if Baal, then follow him. And the people answered him not a word. (1 Kings 18:21)

No man can serve two masters: for either he will hate the one, and love the other; or else he will hold to the one, and despise the other. Ye cannot serve God and mammon.
(Matthew 6:24)

And they said, We will call the damsel, and enquire at her mouth. And they called Rebekah, and said unto her, Wilt thou go with this man? And she said, I will go. (Genesis 24:57–58)

This is the thing which the Lord doth command concerning the daughters of Zelophehad, saying, Let them marry to whom they think best; only to the family of the tribe of their father shall they marry. (Numbers 36:6)

Human beings are admonished to marry after their kind; that is, they are to marry other human beings. There is no scripture encouraging individuals to marry an animal, insect, or inanimate object.

> *Be ye not unequally yoked together with unbelievers: for what fellowship hath righteousness with unrighteousness? and what communion hath light with darkness? And what concord hath Christ with Belial? or what part hath he that believeth with an infidel? And what agreement hath the temple of God with idols? for ye are the temple of the living God; as God hath said, I will dwell in them, and walk in them; and I will be their God, and they shall be my people.* (2 Corinthians 6:14–16)

Scriptural principles encourage individual believers to marry those who are of the same scriptural belief system as they are. Of course, marriage has many different kinds of challenges. If spouses have the same scriptural belief system, this is one challenge the couple doesn't have to deal with.

In fact, having the same belief system provides a very necessary platform and strength that enhances the marriage relationship. Even though individuals may be on varying levels of scriptural understanding, they at least demonstrate confidence in the Holy Scriptures.

The apostle Paul had to address the Christians in the Corinthian church who had spouses with different belief systems. These were couples of whom one of the spouses became a follower of Jesus Christ. Paul encouraged those individuals not to make a hasty departure from that spouse who did not want to follow Jesus Christ.

Paul indicated that the believing spouse is in a good position to influence the unbelieving spouse to turn from a spiritually destructive lifestyle to a spiritually healthy lifestyle by placing faith in Jesus Christ.

I've had the privilege of counseling biracial engaged couples and biracial married couples. During my sessions with them, even if it causes tension, I try to discuss many of the challenges they will face domestically (within their family group), socially (aligning themselves with other couples), environmentally (that which entails community living), culturally (the different nuances and differences within ethnic groups) and even culinary (types of food and their preparation). The only time I suggest that a couple delay their wedding is if there's an issue the couples reveal to be unresolvable via the marriage counseling process.

3

Husband, Love Your Wife

Some years ago during my conversation with a disgruntled husband, he mentioned his future intentions with another wife should his fractured marriage fail altogether. He explained to me the kind of husband he would be. He said in essence, "I would express love with my hands, eyes, words, feet, and ears by treating her with kindness, tenderness, understanding, and sincere expressions of love through bouquets of flowers, cards, and candy."

I stopped him and asked him why he wasn't applying these expressions in his current marital relationship. He became silent. I said that these could very well be the expressions that pull his current marriage relationship from fracture to health if he would be willing to implement them. He was purposely holding these types of expressions back because he thought his wife was not responding in an acceptable manner.

A biblical conclusion concerning a wife is that she possesses all the qualities that the man desires in a woman. The challenge is that he must also be willing to *discover* those qualities by loving her, protecting her, providing for her, and supporting her in such a way that she will rock his world.

In short, she would be the entire woman that he would ever need. When God presented Eve to Adam, she and he were completely naked, symbolically stating that Eve was all Adam needed for love and happiness. Adam's responsibility was to accept and appreciate in a tangible way God's gift of Eve to him.

Loving one's wife should be the foundational principle that the marriage relationship is built upon. Sadly, some people struggle to incorporate this principle. The extra longing of the human heart is fulfilled only by God. Some people seek to fulfill this area on the human level. No one can love us as God does and no one can be the sort of friend to us that God is.

*"Love is an act of endless forgiveness,
a tender look which becomes a habit"*
(Peter Ustinov).

*"Love doesn't make the world go around—
love is what makes the ride worthwhile"*
(Franklin P. Jones).

*"Love is the greatest gift when given.
It is the highest honor when received"*
(Fawn Weaver).

As men we each do whatever is necessary to convince a lady that she should become our girlfriend and subsequently our wife. But after the newness wears off, we began to treat our wife less tenderly.

The attitude that we displayed to win her hand in marriage becomes cloudy and in some cases a distant memory. Love cannot remain in the abstract. Love must be demonstrated sincerely and in tangible activities. The beneficial activities that a man engages in to convince a woman to be his girlfriend and subsequently to marry him must be revisited time and time again to continue to draw her to his side as a loving wife.

The scriptural principle stated below carries significant weight for the success of the marriage relationship:

> *Husbands, love your wives, even as Christ also loved the church, and gave himself for it.*
> (Ephesians 5:25)

The Greek idea of *love* includes the unconditional aspect of this virtue. This is a major key to a successful marriage. *The image of God in man expressing itself to the woman and the image of God in the woman receiving such expression is like kinetic energy.* (Kinetic energy is the energy of mass in motion.)

The kinetic energy of an object is the energy it has because of its motion. The more a man loves his wife and the more a wife responds to her husband is a recipe that keeps the marriage relationship fire burning brightly. The law of reciprocity in social psychology is a social norm of responding to a positive action with another positive action, rewarding kind actions. As a social construct, reciprocity means that in response to friendly actions, people are frequently much nicer and much more cooperative.

Two key words in the above scripture stand out as a turnkey to the kind of love to be exercised by a husband for his wife. Those two words are *even as*. Christ loved the church so much that He died to bring it into existence. Husbands must do no less. But until that ultimate sacrifice is demanded, a husband must follow Jesus' example of how to interact with the object of his love.

- The husband is to position himself between his wife and whatever is causing her frustration.

- The husband is to lovingly lead his wife to a closer relationship with Christ by way of example.

- A truly loving husband will regard his wife as an equal partner in everything that concerns their lives.

- Loving leadership affirms, defers, shares, encourages, and stimulates.

- Loving leadership delights to delegate without demanding.

Below are some of the characteristics of Jesus' love for people (the church), of which husbands are admonished to follow to maintain a healthy marriage relationship with their wives:

1. Don't condemn her.

God sent not his Son into the world to condemn the world; but that the world through him might be saved. (John 3:17)

People can find faults in others whether real or imagined. If you can find something wrong with a person, certainly you can also find something right. By humiliating someone in this fashion, you're also disrespecting the image of God within him or her.

A spouse cannot become what his or her spouse imagines him or her to be. In any area of the human dynamic, there will always be developmental processes. *Condemn* includes the meaning of declaring someone or something as unfit, unworthy, evil, or beyond hope. As humans beings we cannot see the end of a person's life to place on him or her these tags or not. Every person has within him or her the capacity to change, improve, succeed, and contribute.

2. Sacrifice for her.

Therefore doth my Father love me, because I lay down my life, that I might take it again. No man taketh it from me, but I lay it down of

> *myself. I have power to lay it down, and I have power to take it again. This commandment have I received of my Father.* (John 10:17–18)

> *I am the good shepherd: the good shepherd giveth his life for the sheep.* (John 10:11)

A man convinces his fiancé to become his wife and assures her that he will take good care of her no matter what comes or goes. The word *sacrifice* means "to give up something for something else." Tragically, sacrifice on the part of the man often diminishes, leaving the wife feeling deceived.

3. Let her become your best friend.

> *Henceforth I call you not servants; for the servant knoweth not what his lord doeth: but I have called you friends; for all things that I have heard of my Father I have made known unto you. Ye have not chosen me, but I have chosen you, and ordained you, that ye should go and bring forth fruit, and that your fruit should remain: that whatsoever ye shall ask of the Father in my name, he may give it you.*
> (John 15:15–16)

A popular comedian said, "I have my wife and I have a best friend. I share information with my best friend that I don't share with my wife." How horrible to follow this mind-set! If anyone is to be intimate with a husband's deepest thoughts, is should be his wife. When it is said and done, the wife, not the best friend, will be deeply affected if the marriage relationship is impacted.

4. Minister to her spiritual needs.

> *The Spirit of the Lord is upon me, because he hath anointed me to preach the gospel to the poor; he hath sent me to heal the brokenhearted, to preach deliverance to the captives, and recovering of sight to the blind, to set at liberty them that are bruised.* (Luke 4:18)

A husband should meet the physical needs of his wife. Yet there is another side of the woman that should not be neglected—her spiritual side or her relationship with God. It is true that no one favors being pushed into doing something. Therefore, a man must lead by example the scriptural qualities that produce a healthy relationship with God for the spiritual development of his wife.

5. Don't abandon her.

> *He that is an hireling, and not the shepherd, whose own the sheep are not, seeth the wolf coming, and leaveth the sheep, and fleeth: and the wolf catcheth them, and scattereth the sheep. The hireling fleeth, because he is an hireling, and careth not for the sheep.* (John 10:12–13)

I have seen in my short life too many husbands who simply walked away from their responsibility to provide and protect their wives and families. It is my understanding that a woman enters into a marriage relationship with the idea that she would be married for the remainder of her life.

It has been my experience during counseling to discover that wives frequently endure short-term abandonment, especially when the wife is dealing with challenges associated with the marriage relationship.

I once had the unhappy privilege of counseling a sixty-five-year-old dear lady who shared with me that her husband looked her in the face and said, "I never loved you." She began crying and asked why he didn't tell her this when she was much younger. This is very cruel and should never have happened.

6. Understand her.

I am the good shepherd, and know my sheep, and am known of mine. (John 10:14)

In order for a man to understand a woman, he must be willing to listen to her. He must be willing to allow his wife to teach him how she would like to be treated. Men have a basic understanding of the nuances of women from observation. Yet there is nothing that compares to the day-to-day interaction with a wife as she navigates through the vicissitudes of life.

7. Let her know that you "have her back."

I am the vine, ye are the branches: He that abideth in me, and I in him, the same bringeth forth much fruit: for without me ye can do nothing. (John 15:5)

Apart from a word from God, the greatest encourager to a wife is her husband. Of course, a woman can survive and thrive on her own. Yet within the marriage relationship words take on entirely new life-or-death meanings.

It is the husband's responsibility to operate in the kind of love that mirrors Christ's love for the church. It is very important for a husband to defend his wife not only to strangers but also to family members.

I have had the opportunity to counsel married couples in which the wives felt that their husbands' families were ganging up on them. The marital stress came not so much from what their husbands' families were doing but from what their *husbands* were *not* doing in their defense.

> **Marriage is the joining together of two imperfect people.**
>
> **Marriage is the joining together of two broken people.**
>
> **When *broken* cannot be healed, it can be loved.**

Husbands love your wives, and be not bitter against them. (Colossians 3:19)

My little children, let us not love in word, neither in tongue; but in deed and in truth.
(1 John 3:18)

When you think about it, a husband should naturally love his wife. The apostle Paul had to issue a command to men to love their wives. Being bitter by definition is being intensely unpleasant. I once told a young man, "Your bitterness stims from the fact that you didn't marry yourself."

As men we have been created to be tough and resilient in order to provide for and protect our wives and children. Husbands can unwisely turn their toughness and resilience from their intended purposes to disrespecting their wives and mismanaging their households. As noted earlier, many married couples struggle with the simple reality that the persons they married are in many ways different from them.

4

Individuality vs. Individualism

Individuality is not individualism. Individuality is that which distinguishes one person from another. The concept of individualism states that all rights, values, and duties have their origin in the individual. The Holy Scriptures reveal that an individual's rights, values, and duties emerge from God the Father, Son, and Holy Spirit.

When this difference is understood and embraced, then each person can freely contribute to the relationship without fear of being rejected because he or she has a different position. It is true that the goal is to be amenable in order to move forward. Each person in the marriage relationship should recognize, and be recognized, as being unique.

Greek philosopher Protagoras said, "Man is the measure of all things." Today this view holds that man is the ultimate standard by which all life is measured and judged. This means that law, justice, good, beauty, right, and wrong all are to be judged by manmade rules with no credence to either God or the Bible.

The *Dictionary of Philosophy* states that the individual is the ultimate source of value and is dedicated to fostering the individual's creative and moral development in a meaningful and rational way without reference to concepts of the supernatural (God).

If human beings were products of random chance and not intelligent design, this would free mankind from any repercussions after death. Equally so, people could claim that whatever their actions, good or bad, they are predisposed to those actions, which are out of their control.

The Holy Scriptures indicate that God has written the moral concept (right and wrong) within each individual and requires accountability within this life, which will have ramifications in the afterlife.

> *But this shall be the covenant that I will make with the house of Israel; After those days, saith the Lord, I will put my law in their inward parts, and write it in their hearts; and will be their God, and they shall be my people.*
> (Jeremiah 31:33)

> *"(For when the Gentiles, which have not the law, do by nature the things contained in the law, these, having not the law, are a law unto*

themselves. Which shew the work of the law written in their hearts, their conscience also bearing witness, and their thoughts the mean while accusing or else excusing one another;) In the day when God shall judge the secrets of men by Jesus Christ according to my gospel."
(Romans 2:14–16)

For the children being not yet born, neither having done any good or evil, that the purpose of God according to election might stand, not of works, but of him that calleth. (Romans 9:11)

The moral concept of right and wrong is latent within every child. *Latent,* according to Siri, means "that which is existing but not yet developed or manifest; hidden or concealed."

Yes, it is true that everyone has his or her own individual identification characteristics, that is, those identifiers that validate the authenticity of the individual. God did not cookie-cut human beings. We all stand alone as unique. Even identical twins have revealed differences.

Mankind's individuality is not given to confine people to lives of solitude but rather to provide the ability to add value, perspective, and interdependency. The God-given privilege of a man and woman to spend the remainder of his or her life with the other in the holy estate of matrimony is one of God's highest honors.

> *Whoso findeth me findeth life, and shall obtain favour of the Lord.* (Proverbs 8:35)

The verse above reveals that the individual is searching for something other than himself or herself. Even though a man or woman has to discovery or realize who he or she is, meeting each other opens a world of insights, possibilities, mystery, conflict, revelation, comfort, support, inspiration, satisfaction, and more. There is so much that a woman doesn't know about a man; also, there is so much that a man doesn't know about a woman. This makes the marriage relationship a genuine adventure.

The word *find* means "to come upon by searching, to encounter, to meet, to discover, to make a statement." When this experience happens to a man, God has already decreed him *favor*, which means "approval, attention, leniency, permission, grace, special privilege, support, or advantage."

From the moment a man marries, God will begin navigating special opportunities, adventures, wealth, prosperity, and success to the husband that would not have come to him in any other way. Special benefits to him are a direct result of his being married. I frequently tell husbands that for any achievement that's credited to them, they should turn to their wives and say, "It's all because of you."

> *Likewise, ye husbands, dwell with them according to knowledge, giving honour unto the wife, as unto the weaker vessel, and as being heirs*

together of the grace of life; that your prayers be not hindered. (1 Peter 3:7)

Some couples approach marriage from the standpoint of limited knowledge that they think is complete. Listed below are some of these limited concepts:

1. I am a man and she is a woman; nothing else is necessary.
2. Some things will develop naturally.
3. My mom taught me how to be a woman; therefore, I know how to care for a man and a family.
4. I'm just going to do what my dad did.
5. Marriage is not that complicated.
6. When you think about it, having enough money will take care of everything.
7. If we love each other, everything else will work itself out.
8. Give him what he wants and he'll be just fine.
9. Give her what she wants and she'll be just fine.
10. Whom God has joined together no one can separate.
11. He is a Christian and she is a Christian. What more is needed?
12. I can cook and he has a job. It's all good.
13. All we need are the Holy Scriptures.

14. If things don't work out we'll find someone else.
15. If it is to be, nothing can stop it. If it is not to be, nothing can sustain it.
16. I read a book about marriage.
17. I never liked to read.
18. I learn about marriage from watching television.
19. We have both been married before.
20. One of the spouses has been married before.

Countless books are available that deal with the subject of marriage, divorce, and remarriage. Most marriages fail because of a lack of knowledge. This concept is echoed in the book of Hosea 4:6—"My people are destroyed for lack of knowledge."

The more a person educates himself or herself about marriage the more successful the marriage will become. The purpose of a spouse acquiring more knowledge about marriage is not to stockpile information to hurl at his or her spouse but rather to equip himself or herself to be a more complete husband or wife. Marriage is too serious to just wing it. The successful marriage relationship must be filled with intentionality.

Because the marriage relationship is lived out in narrowed proximity, both parties of necessity must mature and without fail work on their faults—or else these negative qualities will become more pronounced.

When Peter, who was a married man (see proof text below), said to honor the wife as the weaker vessel, he was referencing functionality. Functionality is the quality of being suited to serve a purpose well; practicality is the purpose that something is designed or expected to fulfill.

The woman is not weak, but her contribution to the family structure has a softer or tenderer role. Also, her physical strength is different from the strength of a man.

Married men should never forget that their wives are stronger than they think, smarter than they think, more secure than they think, capable of self-support—and set themselves in a certain position in the family structure only to allow their husbands room to grow into their position.

> *And when Jesus was come into Peter's house, he saw his wife's mother laid, and sick of a fever. And he touched her hand, and the fever left her: and she arose, and ministered unto them.*
> (Matthew 8:14–15)

Don't compare your love story to those you watch in movies or television. They are written by screenwriters. Yours can be written by God.

To the world you may be one person, but to one person you may be the world.

> *Let her be as the loving hind and pleasant roe; let her breasts satisfy thee at all times; and be thou ravished always with her love.*
> (Proverbs 5:19)

Ravished: to be overcome with emotion

I have yet to hear a married woman say, "I wish my husband would stop acting as if he can't go on with life without me. My husband shows me way too much attention. If he tells me one more time that he loves me, I'm going to explode!"

"The most desired gift of love is not diamonds, roses or chocolate. It's focused attention" (Rick Warren).

"A happy man married the girl he loves; a happier man loves the girl he married" (Susan Douglas).

"Love put the fun in together, the sad in apart, and the joy in a heart" (unknown).

"Love says, 'The only place I want to be with you is closer'" (unknown).

Love will always find its way back to arms of love.

> *Live joyfully with the wife whom thou lovest all the days of the life of thy vanity, which he hath given thee under the sun, all the days of thy vanity: for that is thy portion in this life, and in thy labour which thou takest under the sun.*
> (Ecclesiastes 9:9)

For this cause shall a man leave father and mother, and shall cleave to his wife: and they twain shall be one flesh? Wherefore they are no more twain, but one flesh. What therefore God hath joined together, let not man put asunder.
(Matthew 19:5–6)

For this cause shall a man leave his father and mother, and shall be joined unto his wife, and they two shall be one flesh. This is a great mystery: but I speak concerning Christ and the church. Nevertheless let every one of you in particular so love his wife even as himself; and the wife see that she reverence her husband.
(Ephesians 5:31–33)

5

Some Revelations Men Should Have About Women

The following are some observations about women from the writings of James C. Dobson:

- **Women encounter problems and pressures that are less common among men.**
- **Loneliness for adult companionship is particularly prevalent for the woman who remains at home.**
- **Women experience deep, persistent yearnings for human contact.**
- **Women long for laughter, love, and romantic moments from their younger days.**
- **A woman's daily dedication to soap operas on television reflects her need to be involved in the lives of people.**
- **Women face moments when they would like to run away from their families.**

- Women have to live with the negative symbolism of being stay-at-home moms as unfulfillment, inferiority, and insignificance.

- Women at times are faced with the inability to explain their feelings to their husbands.

- Women do not like it when their husbands tune them out or listen to them halfheartedly.

- Some women consider men to be lower than snakes with the mentality of a dog.

- Women experience an almost unidentifiable feeling of discouragement on a regular basis.

- For many women low self-esteem is a major problem. No one can stand the awful knowledge that he or she is not needed.

- Women experience a decline in self-respect among themselves.

- Sometimes women feel less intelligent and even stupid. Women value beauty over intelligence.

- The pain that women feel concerning inferiority is incredibly intense and demands the attention of the sufferer.

- Many women suffer from fatigue and time pressure.

- Vance Lombardi said, "Fatigue makes cowards of us all."

- A popular saying seen in various places of business states, "As soon as the rush is over, I am going to have a nervous breakdown. I have earned it, I deserve it, and nobody is going to keep me from it."

- Women can tolerate stress and pressure when they're assured that their spouses know and understand.

- Women feel worthy when they are loved.

- Women yearn to be the special sweethearts of their men, being respected and appreciated and loved with tenderness.

- Women want to teach their spouses their needs, which would reignite the fires of romance.

- Women need emotional fulfillment.

- Women are very open to their spouses' warmth and tenderness.

Marriage is a picture of God's desire to be close to each individual if he or she asks and accepts.

Just like being born, a person has the experience and later the understanding. The same is true about being born again—we have the experience and later the understanding. So it is with marriage. We embrace the experience and over time we get the understanding. Married couples discover ways of drawing closer and closer to each other.

They are mirroring God's promise "I will never leave you or forsake you." A marriage relationship is be a shining example of the love that God has for people. Individuals should be able to look at the type of relationship between married couples and be compelled by what they see to become disciples of Jesus Christ.

> *Let your conversation be without covetousness; and be content with such things as ye have: for he hath said, I will never leave thee, nor forsake thee.* (Hebrews 13:5)

> *Arise, shine; for thy light is come, and the glory of the Lord is risen upon thee.* (Isaiah 60:1)

> *Let your light so shine before men, that they may see your good works, and glorify your Father which is in heaven.* (Matthew 5:16)

> *And the lord said unto the servant, Go out into the highways and hedges, and compel them to come in, that my house may be filled.* (Luke 14:23)

Some individuals choose not to get married and some individuals feel a divine call to live a lifestyle of being single. Yet many individuals desire to get married. That being so, marriage partners should do the necessary work to have healthy marriage relationships. I counsel many couples never to come off their honeymoons. The purpose of getting married is to be *with* each other, not away from each other.

> *For there are some eunuchs, which were so born from their mother's womb: and there are some eunuchs, which were made eunuchs of men: and there be eunuchs, which have made themselves eunuchs for the kingdom of heaven's sake. He that is able to receive it, let him receive it.* (Matthew 19:12)

> *But and if thou marry, thou hast not sinned; and if a virgin marry, she hath not sinned. Nevertheless such shall have trouble in the flesh: but I spare you.* (1 Corinthians 7:28)

The marriage relationship is the axis around which all the family relationships are found.

> *And did not he make one? Yet had he the residue of the spirit. And wherefore one? That he might seek a godly seed. Therefore take heed to your spirit, and let none deal treacherously against the wife of his youth.* (Malachi 2:15)

For the unbelieving husband is sanctified by the wife, and the unbelieving wife is sanctified by the husband: else were your children unclean; but now are they holy. (1 Corinthians 7:14)

"A happy marriage is the union of two good forgivers" (Robert Quillen).

Take heed to yourselves: If thy brother trespass against thee, rebuke him; and if he repent, forgive him. And if he trespass against thee seven times in a day, and seven times in a day turn again to thee, saying, I repent; thou shalt forgive him. (Luke 17:3–4)

And when ye stand praying, forgive, if ye have ought against any: that your Father also which is in heaven may forgive you your trespasses. But if ye do not forgive, neither will your Father which is in heaven forgive your trespasses. (Mark 11:25–26)

Afterward Jesus findeth him in the temple, and said unto him, Behold, thou art made whole: sin no more, lest a worse thing come unto thee. (John 5:14)

When Jesus had lifted up himself, and saw none but the woman, he said unto her, Woman, where

> *are those thine accusers? hath no man condemned thee? She said, No man, Lord. And Jesus said unto her, Neither do I condemn thee: go, and sin no more.* (John 8:10–11)

> *Know ye not, that to whom ye yield yourselves servants to obey, his servants ye are to whom ye obey; whether of sin unto death, or of obedience unto righteousness?* (Romans 6:16)

Tragically, there are individuals who yield themselves to a lifestyle that ultimately destroys their marriage relationship.

"Success in marriage does not come merely through finding the right person but through *being* the right person" (James C. Dobson).

> *Therefore if any man be in Christ, he is a new creature: old things are passed away; behold, all things are become new.* (2 Corinthians 5:17)

> *I am crucified with Christ: nevertheless I live; yet not I, but Christ liveth in me: and the life which I now live in the flesh I live by the faith of the Son of God, who loved me, and gave himself for me.* (Galatians 2:20)

> *For in Christ Jesus neither circumcision availeth anything, nor uncircumcision, but a new creature.* (Galatians 6:15)

"Don't marry the person you think you can live *with*; marry only the individual you think you can't live *without*" (James C. Dobson).

And Jacob loved Rachel; and said, I will serve thee seven years for Rachel thy younger daughter. And Laban said, It is better that I give her to thee, than that I should give her to another man: abide with me. And Jacob served seven years for Rachel; and they seemed unto him but a few days, for the love he had to her.
(Genesis 29:18–20)

"A goal in marriage is not to think alike but to think together" (Robert C. Dodds).

Can two walk together, except they be agreed? (Amos 3:3)

But he, knowing their thoughts, said unto them, Every kingdom divided against itself is brought to desolation; and a house divided against a house falleth. (Luke 11:17)

Be ye not unequally yoked together with unbelievers: for what fellowship hath righteousness with unrighteousness? and what communion hath light with darkness? (2 Corinthians 6:14)

Marriage is shared pain.

And Rebekah said to Isaac, I am weary of my life because of the daughters of Heth: if Jacob take a wife of the daughters of Heth, such as these which are of the daughters of the land, what good shall my life do me? (Genesis 27:46)

And Esau seeing that the daughters of Canaan pleased not Isaac his father; Then went Esau unto Ishmael, and took unto the wives which he had Mahalath the daughter of Ishmael Abraham's son, the sister of Nebajoth, to be his wife. (Genesis 28:8–9)

Marriage is the joining together of two imperfect people.

For all have sinned, and come short of the glory of God. (Romans 3:23)

For there is not a just man upon earth, that doeth good, and sinneth not. (Ecclesiastes 7:20)

If we say that we have no sin, we deceive ourselves, and the truth is not in us. If we confess our sins, he is faithful and just to forgive us our sins, and to cleanse us from all unrighteousness. (1 John 1:8–9)

"In every marriage more than a week old there are grounds for divorce. The challenge is to find and to continue to find grounds to stay married" (Robert Anderson).

Wherefore they are no more twain, but one flesh. What therefore God hath joined together, let not man put asunder. (Matthew 19:6)

I can do all things through Christ which strengtheneth me. (Philippians 4:13)

Abide in me, and I in you. As the branch cannot bear fruit of itself, except it abide in the vine; no more can ye, except ye abide in me. I am the vine, ye are the branches: He that abideth in me, and I in him, the same bringeth forth much fruit: for without me ye can do nothing. (John 15:4–5)

In marriage you will experience your greatest hurt and your greatest healing.

And a man lie with her carnally, and it be hid from the eyes of her husband, and be kept close, and she be defiled, and there be no witness against her, neither she be taken with the manner; And the spirit of jealousy come upon him, and he be jealous of his wife, and she be defiled: or if the spirit of jealousy come upon him, and he be jealous of his wife, and she be not defiled. (Numbers 5:13–14)

6

Wife, Love Your Husband

Thank about this quote concerning a lady contemplating her wedding: "I dreamed of a wedding of elaborate elegance, a church filled with family and friends. I asked him what kind of wedding he wanted. He said the one that would make you my wife."

In the book of Genesis after Adam and Eve disobeyed God's instruction not to eat from the tree in the middle of the garden, God had to issue punitive instructions.

> *Unto the woman he said, I will greatly multiply thy sorrow and thy conception; in sorrow thou shalt bring forth children; and thy desire shall be to thy husband, and he shall rule over thee.* (Genesis 3:16)

Alfred Adler said, "What people want most of all is power"—not the kind of power that helps another person to develop but the kind that dominates. The husband's rule over his wife should not be humiliating, domineering, punitive, controlling, or disrespectful. If a husband loves his wife as Christ loves the church, all is well.

The husband is to understand and acknowledge his wife's gifts, desires, goals, and creativity and help guide or manage circumstances, situations to help her achieve those objectives. The downside is that many husbands inject the wrong motivation, which hinders, discourages, and sabotages their spouses' dreams. People in a marriage relationship will not achieve their dreams without the support of each other—because their lives are interwoven.

> *Likewise, ye wives, be in subjection to your own husbands; that, if any obey not the word, they also may without the word be won by the conversation of the wives; While they behold your chaste conversation coupled with fear. Whose adorning let it not be that outward adorning of plaiting the hair, and of wearing of gold, or of putting on of apparel; But let it be the hidden man of the heart, in that which is not corruptible, even the ornament of a meek and quiet spirit, which is in the sight of God of great price.* (1 Peter 3:1–4)

Peter is not saying that a woman should not wear makeup or do things to enhance her external beauty, but rather not to let those external applications become her main recognition points. What is more important is the internal or spiritual qualities that represent the image of God.

Peter indicates that a non-believing husband can be won by the wife's lifestyle rather than her looks or the bombardment of scriptures. An unbelieving husband does not see the heart of a believing wife but rather her outer demonstrations, actions, behavior—the practical embodiment of what she believes.

> *But the Lord said unto Samuel, Look not on his countenance, or on the height of his stature; because I have refused him: for the Lord seeth not as man seeth; for man looketh on the outward appearance, but the Lord looketh on the heart.*
> (1 Samuel 16:7)

> *The aged women likewise, that they be in behaviour as becometh holiness, not false accusers, not given to much wine, teachers of good things; That they may teach the young women to be sober, to love their husbands, to love their children, To be discreet, chaste, keepers at home, good, obedient to their own husbands, that the word of God be not blasphemed.*
> (Titus 2:3–5)

Some people are laboring under the understanding that if a wife is a stay-at home mom, she has missed her real purpose in life. If the family income will allow and the wife and husband are willing, it is not a criminal offense to stay at home and raise children to be self-aware, self-confident, successful, and productive citizens of society.

It is also not a criminal act if both spouses are active income providers and incorporate the usage of a child care facility. Yet it is still incumbent on the parents to make sure that their children are presented with healthy spiritual development from the Word of God and a safe, secure environment.

> *Wives, submit yourselves unto your own husbands, as it is fit in the Lord.*
> (Colossians 3:18)

> *Submitting yourselves one to another in the fear of God. Wives, submit yourselves unto your own husbands, as unto the Lord.*
> (Ephesians 5:21–22)

> *Nevertheless let every one of you in particular so love his wife even as himself; and the wife see that she reverence* [honor] *her husband.*
> (Ephesians 5:33)

> *But I would have you know, that the head of every man is Christ; and the head of the woman is the man; and the head of Christ is God.*
> (1 Corinthians 11:3)

Some husbands think that only the wife is to submit to authority. The apostle Paul said that submission must come from both the husband *and* the wife. There is a level of authority that both spouses inherit by virtue of being married.

When this kind of curtesy is given and received, the marriage relationship is strengthened. When a husband loves his wife as unto the Lord, the wife's road to submission is made easy because she knows that her husband has her best interests in mind in which she reverences (honors) him.

The *headship* of the man refers to functionality. Both the husband and wife are *co-regents* (those who govern a kingdom in the minority, absence, or disability of the sovereign; those who rule or reign).

The airline carriers I have traveled with always have copilots. A copilot is a qualified pilot who assists or relieves the pilot but is not ultimately in command. Both pilots are equally skilled in flying the aircraft and rely upon each other for the success of the flight and safety of the passengers. So it is with the husband and wife.

The husband and wife must work together to achieve the business aspect of the home and the well-being of their children and themselves. I have learned that the wife has the deciding vote to confirm that the husband is the head of the home, which is predicated on his love for her not only in word but also in demonstration and sincerity.

Jesus taught that if a house is divided against itself it will not stand (see the verse below). That is why it is so necessary for a husband and wife to understand their shared roles and the roles for which they are gifted.

> *And Jesus knew their thoughts, and said unto them, Every kingdom divided against itself is brought to desolation; and every city or house divided against itself shall not stand.*
> (Matthew 12:25)

The wife must be motivated to inspire her husband to lead her to Christ and heaven.

Some Revelations About Men That Women Should Know

Adapted from Beth Moore

Men would rather feel unloved than inadequate and disrespected.

Many men wish their wives wouldn't question their knowledge or argue with their decisions all the time.

Many men confess that they feel that their opinions and decisions are actively valued in every area of their lives except at home.

Some women make the mistake of ordering their husbands around as they do the kids.

Men like to figure things out for themselves, which produces a feeling of accomplishment and affirmation of their manhood.

The phase "I know you can do it" will help one's husband hit a home run.

The woman holds an incredible power in the way she communicates with her husband, to tear him down or to build him up.

The most fragile thing on the planet is a man's ego. When a wife criticizes her husband in private and especially in public, he is crushed.

Even good-natured teasing can sometimes be humiliating.

The only time a guy's guard is completely down is with the woman he loves. So she can pierce his heart as no one else can.

Sometimes women assign unloving motives to their men that could actually be traced back to things the women have inadvertently said or done.

Despite their in-control exterior, men often feel like impostors and are insecure, fearing that their inadequacies will be discovered.

Even if the wife made enough income to support the family's lifestyle, it would make no difference to the mental burden the husband feels to be the provider.

A woman's sexual desire for her husband profoundly affects his sense of well-being and confidence in all areas of his life.

Even happily married men struggle with being pulled toward live and recollected images of other women.

Actually, most men enjoy romance and want to be romantic but hesitate because they doubt they can succeed.

A wife doesn't need to be size three, but her man does need to see her making the effort to take care of herself, and he will take on significant cost or inconvenience in order to support her.

A man's heart is touched by a few simple words: "I'm proud of you."

Many men do not actively feel appreciated by their families.

All those women in men's magazines convey one message: "I want you, and you are the most desirable man in the world."

Sex plays a huge role in a man's self-confidence.

Men get frustrated when they feel that their wives are the source of some of the pressure they feel.

A man will internalize his wife's disappointment in him as a personal failure to provide.

Men desire that their wives help to relieve the pressure they feel rather than adding to it.

A wife's sexual desire for her husband salves a deep sense of loneliness.

At the basic level a man wants to be wanted.

A man wants to be loved for who he is and not for who his wife wants him to be.

If a man is teased by his wife about not getting something right, he will not try it again for some time.

A woman who is doing things with her husband is considered incredibly attractive.

A man wants to know that his wife is comfortable in her skin. If this is the case, extra pounds are not noticed.

Men are not completely truthful even if their wives want the truth. Most men are conditioned to withhold how they truly feel about a matter.

A man loves his wife with all his heart and would do anything to keep that love alive, even if it crosses legal lines.

The Bridge of the One-Hundred-Percent Principle

It's has been said in many venues that marriage is to be lived out at one-hundred-percent participation. The husband is to give fifty percent and the wife is to give fifty percent. The danger of each party being responsible for fifty percent of the marriage success adds to one hundred percent of its failure. If either spouse stumbles in some fashion and is therefore unable to give his or her fifty percent, which is inevitable, the bridge across the valley to a resolution becomes impassible.

> *But now thus saith the Lord that created thee, O Jacob, and he that formed thee, O Israel, Fear not: for I have redeemed thee, I have called thee by thy name; thou art mine. When thou passest through the waters, I will be with thee; and through the rivers, they shall not overflow thee: when thou walkest through the fire, thou shalt not be burned; neither shall the flame kindle upon thee.* (Isaiah 43:1–2)

> *I returned, and saw under the sun, that the race is not to the swift, nor the battle to the strong, neither yet bread to the wise, nor yet riches to men of understanding, nor yet favour to men of skill; but time and chance happeneth to them all.* (Ecclesiastes 9:11)

Now if each person in the marriage relationship gives one hundred percent, it is like a bridge reaching from one side of a hundred-foot valley to the other side. As both the husband and wife give one hundred percent to the success of the marriage relationship, each can flow back and forward solving problems that keep the marriage relationship healthy. If either spouse hits the wall and is unable to give one hundred percent to the relationship, the solvability of the marital issue is high because of the one hundred percent of the other spouse.

If the bridge to reach the other side is in place, either spouse can cross over, either to offer loving support or to become the recipient of loving support. The wife wants not only to *know* that her husband loves her but also to *feel* that her husband loves her. The husband wants to know that his wife is appreciative of his efforts to protect and support her.

Listed are some insights from Emerson Eggerichs that will help married couples build bridges from the one-hundred-percent commitment concept. Some are directed to the husband, some to the wife, and some to both spouses.

1. Listen and be able to repeat back what she said.
2. Tell him you are thankful for his strength and being able to lean on him.
3. Don't try to fix her problems unless she specifically asks for a solution.
4. Support his self-image as a leader.
5. Try to identify her feelings.

6. Never say, "You are responsible," but "We are still equal."
7. Never dismiss her feelings, regardless of how illogical they may seem to you.
8. Praise his good decisions.
9. Say, "I appreciate your sharing that with me."
10. Be gracious if he makes a bad decision.
11. Don't interrupt her when she's trying to tell you how she feels.
12. Disagree with him only in private.
13. Apologize and admit when you are wrong and ask for forgiveness.
14. Honor his authority in front of the kids.
15. Express appreciation for all she does.
16. Give your disagreement but never challenge his right to lead.
17. Try to keep your relationship up to date.
18. Don't play head games with him.
19. Resolve the unresolved; never just say, "Forget it."
20. Never nurse bitterness and always reassure your spouse of your love.
21. Pray *with* her and *for* her, especially after a hurtful time.

7

Sexual Integrity Principles

According to *Psychology Today*, "Men are somewhat different than women when it comes to cheating and a lot of that difference arises from the fact that men tend to define infidelity rather loosely. . . . More generally, most men would say that utilizing porn as a sexual outlet while in a primary, committed relationship is not cheating."

If the question were asked of men's wives, fiancés, or girlfriends, "Is porn cheating?" it would be discovered that many women do indeed explore sexual activity that does not include their husbands, fiancés or boyfriends. If the question were asked of women's husbands, fiancés, or boyfriends, "Is this exploration cheating?" it would be revealed that individuals who self-justify this type of activity often do it in secrecy because the looming reality is that it may be viewed as unfavorable and indicative of infidelity.

Infidelity in a marriage context is willful unfaithfulness to a moral obligation or breaking vows stated during a religious or civil ceremony, which include a promise to remain sexually faithful.

The Scriptures are replete with positive principles that are resources for men and women who are determined to honor God with their bodies. God is the one who created sex and the desire within males and females to have sexual intercourse. In order to understand the purpose of something created, the first logical step is to contact the Creator. I have discovered that God is not trying to stop mankind from sexual intercourse; rather, He is trying to help people understand the condition under which this act can occur.

I am familiar with several men who brag about the number of women they impregnated. Some go to great lengths to tell a woman what she longs to hear just to have sex with her. As a man moves on to his next sexual conquest, the woman is left with emotional issues and possibly in nine months the responsibility of being a single parent. Two lives are disrupted, those of the mother and the child, not to mention the different kinds of sexually transmitted diseases.

I have seen several movies featuring runaway trains. In each one the train personnel scramble to get control of the train, of course, because of the potential damage that can occur. The goal is to regain control without damaging the train itself or the tracks. The lyrics of a song succinctly say, "I don't mind being the other woman as long as I know that I'm the *only* other woman." It has been said that art imitates life. It is utterly tragic that a man or woman would treat in such a way the body that God allowed him or her to experience.

This is precisely why we need to stay connected to the Creator to gain a better understanding of His purpose for His creation. Just as with a runaway train, a man or woman having out-of-control sex will inevitably cause harm to himself or herself and others.

> *This is the will of God, even your sanctification, that ye should abstain from fornication: That every one of you should know how to possess his vessel in sanctification and honour; Not in the lust of concupiscence, even as the Gentiles which know not God.* (1 Thessalonians 4:3–5)

> *Flee fornication. Every sin that a man doeth is without the body; but he that committeth fornication sinneth against his own body.*
> (1 Corinthians 6:18)

> *Let not sin therefore reign in your mortal body, that ye should obey it in the lusts thereof. Neither yield ye your members as instruments of unrighteousness unto sin: but yield yourselves unto God, as those that are alive from the dead, and your members as instruments of righteousness unto God.* (Romans 6:12–13)

> *I speak after the manner of men because of the infirmity of your flesh: for as ye have yielded your members servants to uncleanness and to iniquity*

unto iniquity; even so now yield your members servants to righteousness unto holiness. (Romans 6:19)

Know ye not that your bodies are the members of Christ? shall I then take the members of Christ, and make them the members of an harlot? God forbid. (1 Corinthians 6:15)

Mortify therefore your members which are upon the earth; fornication, uncleanness, inordinate affection, evil concupiscence, and covetousness, which is idolatry. (Colossians 3:5)

I beseech you therefore, brethren, by the mercies of God, that ye present your bodies a living sacrifice, holy, acceptable unto God, which is your reasonable service. (Romans 12:1)

According to my earnest expectation and my hope, that in nothing I shall be ashamed, but that with all boldness, as always, so now also Christ shall be magnified in my body, whether it be by life, or by death. (Philippians 1:20)

Marriage is honourable in all, and the bed undefiled: but whoremongers and adulterers God will judge. (Hebrews 13:4)

Ten Reasons Men Cheat
(from www.psychologytoday.com)
with Scriptural Rebuttals

1. **He's a liar.** He never intended to be monogamous despite his commitment. This man views monogamy as something to be worked around rather than embraced.

> *Why is my pain perpetual, and my wound incurable, which refuseth to be healed? wilt thou be altogether unto me as a liar, and as waters that fail?* (Jeremiah 15:18)

> *Ye are of your father the devil, and the lusts of your father ye will do. He was a murderer from the beginning, and abode not in the truth, because there is no truth in him. When he speaketh a lie, he speaketh of his own: for he is a liar, and the father of it.* (John 8:44)

2. **He's insecure**. Deep down he feels that he is too young, too old, too fat, too thin, too poor, too stupid or too *whatever* to be desirable. He uses flirtation.

> *For the Lord shall be thy confidence and shall keep thy foot from being taken.*
> (Proverbs 3:26)

> *In the fear of the Lord is strong confidence: and his children shall have a place of refuge.*
> (Proverbs 14:26)

> *Confidence in an unfaithful man in time of trouble is like a broken tooth, and a foot out of joint.* (Proverbs 25:19)

3. **He's immature.** He thinks that as long as his partner doesn't find out, he isn't hurting anybody. He doesn't realize that he *will* be discovered.

> *When I was a child, I spake as a child, I understood as a child, I thought as a child: but when I became a man, I put away childish things.* (1 Corinthians 13:11)

> *Brethren, be not children in understanding: howbeit in malice be ye children, but in understanding be men.* (1 Corinthians 14:20)

4. **He's damaged.** Perhaps he's acting out early trauma (physical abuse, neglect, or sexual abuse) possibly to self-medicate (escape from) his emotional and psychological pain.

> *The Lord is nigh unto them that are of a broken heart; and saveth such as be of a contrite spirit.* (Psalm 34:18)

> *The Spirit of the Lord is upon me, because he hath anointed me to preach the gospel to the*

> *poor; he hath sent me to heal the brokenhearted, to preach deliverance to the captives, and recovering of sight to the blind, to set at liberty them that are bruised, To preach the acceptable year of the Lord.* (Luke 4:18–19)

5. **He has unreasonable expectations.** He believes that his spouse should meet his every sexual and emotional need, 24/7, without fail.

> *Wives submit yourselves unto your own husbands, as it is fit in the Lord. Husbands love your wives, and be not bitter against them.*
> (Colossians 3:18–19)

6. **He's bored.** When his spouse inevitably fails him (in his view) he feels entitled to seek intimate attention elsewhere. Maybe he wants more attention from his mate and thinks a period of pulling away will cause her to comply.

> *Let thy fountain be blessed: and rejoice with the wife of thy youth. Let her be as the loving hind and pleasant roe; let her breasts satisfy thee at all times; and be thou ravished always with her love. And why wilt thou, my son, be ravished with a strange woman, and embrace the bosom of a stranger?* (Proverbs 5:18–20)

7. **He's confused about love.** He does not understand that in truly loving relationships, the early, visceral attraction is gradually replaced by sweeter feelings of longer-term honesty, commitment, and emotional intimacy.

> *God is not the author of confusion, but of peace, as in all churches of the saints.*
> (1 Corinthians 14:33)

> *And be not conformed to this world: but be ye transformed by the renewing of your mind, that ye may prove what is that good, and acceptable, and perfect, will of God.* (Romans 12:2)

> *The eyes of your understanding being enlightened; that ye may know what is the hope of his calling, and what the riches of the glory of his inheritance in the saints.* (Ephesians 1:18)

> *Put off concerning the former conversation the old man, which is corrupt according to the deceitful lusts; And be renewed in the spirit of your mind.* (Ephesians 4:22–23)

8. **He's addicted**. He may be laboring under a controlling substance. He may also have an issue with sexual compulsivity, meaning he uses sexual activity to self-soothe and escape uncomfortable emotions.

Let us hear the conclusion of the whole matter: Fear God, and keep his commandments: for this is the whole duty of man. For God shall bring every work into judgment, with every secret thing, whether it be good, or whether it be evil. (Ecclesiastes 12:13–14)

I beseech you, brethren, (ye know the house of Stephanas, that it is the firstfruits of Achaia, and that they have addicted themselves to the ministry of the saints,) That ye submit yourselves unto such, and to every one that helpeth with us, and laboureth. (1 Corinthians 16:15–16)

Flee also youthful lusts: but follow righteousness, faith, charity, peace, with them that call on the Lord out of a pure heart. (2 Timothy 2:22)

I keep under my body and bring it into subjection: lest that by any means, when I have preached to others, I myself should be a castaway. (1 Corinthians 9:27)

9. **He wants out.** He's looking to end his current relationship and using external sexual and romantic activities to give his wife or girlfriend the message indirectly.

Yet ye say, Wherefore? Because the Lord hath been witness between thee and the wife of thy youth, against whom thou hast dealt treacherously: yet is she thy companion, and the wife of thy covenant. (Malachi 2:14)

And he answered and said unto them, Have ye not read, that he which made them at the beginning made them male and female, And said, For this cause shall a man leave father and mother, and shall cleave to his wife: and they twain shall be one flesh? Wherefore they are no more twain, but one flesh. What therefore God hath joined together, let not man put asunder. (Matthew 19:4–6)

10. **He lacks male bonding and a peer community.** Having undervalued his healthy need to maintain solid, supportive friendships and community with other men, a busy or distracted husband is all the more injurious as he expects all his emotional and physical needs to be met by this one person.

A man that hath friends must shew himself friendly: and there is a friend that sticketh closer than a brother. (Proverbs 18:24)

Henceforth I call you not servants; for the servant knoweth not what his lord doeth: but I have called you friends; for all things that I have heard of my Father I have made known unto you. (John 15:15)

That which we have seen and heard declare we unto you, that ye also may have fellowship with us: and truly our fellowship is with the Father, and with his Son Jesus Christ. (1 John 1:3)

Ten Reasons Women Cheat (from psychologytoday.com) with Scriptural Rebuttals

1. **Lack of intimacy.** This could mean anything from kissing to more sexual activity. It's normal for every relationship to decline in intimacy over time, especially in a long-term marriage. Many women have admitted this to be the number-one reason they seek another man on the side. The simple truth is that women, much more than men, feel connected and valued through non-sexual emotional interaction, such as gift-giving, being remembered, and talking.

> *Let the husband render unto the wife due benevolence: and likewise also the wife unto the husband. The wife hath not power of her own body, but the husband: and likewise also the husband hath not power of his own body, but the wife. Defraud ye not one the other, except it be with consent for a time, that ye may give yourselves to fasting and prayer; and come together again, that Satan tempt you not for your incontinency.* (1 Corinthians 7:3–5)

2. **Lack of communication.** Another thing that's normal in a long-term marriage or relationship is the decline of communication. If the wife starts to feel that the relationship has gotten very routine to the point that she and her husband barely speak, she will be much more likely to flirt and even cheat when the opportunity presents itself.

> *And ye shall teach them your children, speaking of them when thou sittest in thine house, and when thou walkest by the way, when thou liest down, and when thou risest up.*
> (Deuteronomy 11:19)

> *My mouth shall shew forth thy righteousness and thy salvation all the day; for I know not the numbers thereof. I will go in the strength of the Lord God: I will make mention of thy righteousness, even of thine only. O God, thou hast taught me from my youth: and hitherto have I declared thy wondrous works. Now also when I am old and greyheaded, O God, forsake me not; until I have shewed thy strength unto this generation, and thy power to every one that is to come.* (Psalms 71:15–18)

> *A wholesome tongue is a tree of life: but perverseness therein is a breach in the spirit.*
> (Proverbs 15:4)

> *A word fitly spoken is like apples of gold in pictures of silver.* (Proverbs 25:11)

3. **Hypersexuality.** While it's not something most people can admit to, it's a real thing. Just like anything else that releases dopamine through the body, sex can become an addition for both men and women.

> *This I say then, Walk in the Spirit, and ye shall not fulfil the lust of the flesh. For the flesh lusteth against the Spirit, and the Spirit against the flesh: and these are contrary the one to the other: so that ye cannot do the things that ye would.*
> (Galatians 5:16–17)

> *That every one of you should know how to possess his vessel in sanctification and honour; Not in the lust of concupiscence, even as the Gentiles which know not God.*
> (1 Thessalonians 4:4–5)

> *But every man is tempted, when he is drawn away of his own lust, and enticed. Then when lust hath conceived, it bringeth forth sin: and sin, when it is finished, bringeth forth death.*
> (James 1:14–15)

> *Love not the world, neither the things that are in the world. If any man love the world, the love of the Father is not in him. For all that is in the world, the lust of the flesh, and the lust of the eyes, and the pride of life, is not of the Father, but is of the world.* (1 John 2:15–16)

4. **They want to check out of the relationship.** Many women are needy for affection. They don't want to leave a relationship unless they already have another one lined up.

> *And the woman which hath an husband that believeth not, and if he be pleased to dwell with her, let her not leave him.*
> (1 Corinthians 7:13)

5. **The married couples have both grown apart.** When a husband and wife start living different lifestyles instead of doing things together, that's a cause for concern. This is what leads them to stray and connect with other people they feel they have common interests with. Sometimes a woman can feel more like a nanny, maid, mother, or financial provider than a wife or girlfriend.

> *And said, For this cause shall a man leave father and mother, and shall cleave to his wife: and they twain shall be one flesh? Wherefore they are no more twain, but one flesh. What therefore God hath joined together, let not man put asunder.*
> (Matthew 19:5–6)

> *So ought men to love their wives as their own bodies. He that loveth his wife loveth himself. For no man ever yet hated his own flesh; but nourisheth and cherisheth it, even as the Lord the church: For we are members of his body, of his flesh, and of his bones. For this cause shall a man leave his father and mother, and shall be joined unto his wife, and they two shall be one flesh.* (Ephesians 5:28–31)

6. **To get revenge.** Some married women will use other men to get back at their husbands for something they did. That something could be anything from finding out that maybe they cheated in the past to reacting to something they found disrespectful.

> *Dearly beloved, avenge not yourselves, but rather give place unto wrath: for it is written, Vengeance is mine; I will repay, saith the Lord.* (Romans 12:19)

7. **Immaturity.** You can boil most infidelity down to this reason alone. Cheating in and of itself is an immature act, regardless of the reason.

> *The aged women likewise, that they be in behaviour as becometh holiness, not false accusers, not given to much wine, teachers of*

> *good things; That they may teach the young women to be sober, to love their husbands, to love their children, To be discreet, chaste, keepers at home, good, obedient to their own husbands, that the word of God be not blasphemed.*
> (Titus 2:3–5)

> *A foolish woman is clamourous: she is simple, and knoweth nothing.* (Proverbs 9:13)

8. **Low self-esteem**. Woman with low self-esteem, depression, unresolved childhood trauma, and other similar issues may seek validation through romantic and sexual activity. If someone wants them in "that way," they feel worthwhile, desirable, wanted, needed, and loveable.

> *So God created man in his own image, in the image of God created he him; male and female created he them. And God blessed them, and God said unto them, Be fruitful, and multiply, and replenish the earth, and subdue it: and have dominion over the fish of the sea, and over the fowl of the air, and over every living thing that moveth upon the earth.* (Genesis 1:27–28)

> *I will praise thee; for I am fearfully and wonderfully made: marvellous are thy works; and that my soul knoweth right well. My*

substance was not hid from thee, when I was made in secret, and curiously wrought in the lowest parts of the earth. Thine eyes did see my substance, yet being unperfect; and in thy book all my members were written, which in continuance were fashioned, when as yet there was none of them. How precious also are thy thoughts unto me, O God! how great is the sum of them! (Psalm 139:14–17)

9. **Lack of female social support.** A big part of healthy womanhood involves supportive female friendships and a sense of female community. Women in this case undervalue female social support and overvalue the attention of men.

> *And they called Rebekah, and said unto her, Wilt thou go with this man? And she said, I will go. And they sent away Rebekah their sister, and her nurse, and Abraham's servant, and his men.* (Genesis 24:58–59)

> *Deborah, Rebekah's nurse died, and she was buried beneath Bethel under an oak: and the name of it was called Allonbachuth.* (Genesis 35:8)

> *The aged women likewise, that they be in behaviour as becometh holiness, not false*

> *accusers, not given to much wine, teachers of good things; That they may teach the young women to be sober, to love their husbands, to love their children, To be discreet, chaste, keepers at home, good, obedient to their own husbands, that the word of God be not blasphemed.*
> (Titus 2:3–5)

> *A friend loveth at all times, and a brother is born for adversity.* (Proverbs 17:17)

> *A man that hath friends must shew himself friendly: and there is a friend that sticketh closer than a brother.* (Proverbs 18:24)

> *Ointment and perfume rejoice the heart: so doth the sweetness of a man's friend by hearty counsel.* (Proverbs 27:9)

10. **Using sex as a step for career advancement or to improve the woman's life status.** Some women think that their career preparation and the process for advancement are slow.

> *And it was told Tamar, saying, Behold thy father in law goeth up to Timnath to shear his sheep. And she put her widow's garments off from her, and covered her with a vail, and wrapped herself, and sat in an open place, which is by the*

way to Timnath; for she saw that Shelah was grown, and she was not given unto him to wife. When Judah saw her, he thought her to be an harlot; because she had covered her face.
(Genesis 38:13–15)

And he turned unto her by the way, and said, Go to, I pray thee, let me come in unto thee; (for he knew not that she was his daughter in law.) And she said, What wilt thou give me, that thou mayest come in unto me? And he said, I will send thee a kid from the flock. And she said, Wilt thou give me a pledge, till thou send it? And he said, What pledge shall I give thee? And she said, Thy signet, and thy bracelets, and thy staff that is in thine hand. And he gave it her, and came in unto her, and she conceived by him.
(Genesis 38:16–18)

And it came to pass afterward, that he loved a woman in the valley of Sorek, whose name was Delilah. And the lords of the Philistines came up unto her, and said unto her, Entice him, and see wherein his great strength lieth, and by what means we may prevail against him, that we may bind him to afflict him; and we will give thee every one of us eleven hundred pieces of silver.
(Judges 16:4–5)

> *And when Delilah saw that he had told her all his heart, she sent and called for the lords of the Philistines, saying, Come up this once, for he hath shewed me all his heart. Then the lords of the Philistines came up unto her, and brought money in their hand. And she made him sleep upon her knees; and she called for a man, and she caused him to shave off the seven locks of his head; and she began to afflict him, and his strength went from him.* (Judges 16:18–19)

Integrity: following moral values or ethical principles; the quality or state of being complete or undivided; honesty; following through with what one promised

> *If any man take a wife, and go in unto her, and hate her, And give occasions of speech against her, and bring up an evil name upon her, and say, I took this woman, and when I came to her, I found her not a maid: Then shall the father of the damsel, and her mother, take and bring forth the tokens of the damsel's virginity unto the elders of the city in the gate: And the damsel's father shall say unto the elders, I gave my daughter unto this man to wife, and he hateth her; And, lo, he hath given occasions of speech against her, saying, I found not thy daughter a maid; and yet these are the tokens of my daughter's virginity. And they shall spread the cloth before the elders of the city.*

And the elders of that city shall take that man and chastise him; And they shall amerce him in an hundred shekels of silver, and give them unto the father of the damsel, because he hath brought up an evil name upon a virgin of Israel: and she shall be his wife; he may not put her away all his days. But if this thing be true, and the tokens of virginity be not found for the damsel: Then they shall bring out the damsel to the door of her father's house, and the men of her city shall stone her with stones that she die: because she hath wrought folly in Israel, to play the whore in her father's house: so shalt thou put evil away from among you.
(Deuteronomy 22:13–21)

In the course of time, Amnon son of David fell in love with Tamar, the beautiful sister of Absalom son of David. Amnon became so obsessed with his sister Tamar that he made himself ill. She was a virgin, and it seemed impossible for him to do anything to her. Now Amnon had an adviser named Jonadab son of Shimeah, David's brother. Jonadab was a very shrewd man. He asked Amnon, "Why do you, the king's son, look so haggard morning after morning? Won't you tell me?"

Amnon said to him, "I'm in love with Tamar, my brother Absalom's sister. "Go to bed

and pretend to be ill," Jonadab said. *"When your father comes to see you, say to him, 'I would like my sister Tamar to come and give me something to eat. Let her prepare the food in my sight so I may watch her and then eat it from her hand.'" So Amnon lay down and pretended to be ill. When the king came to see him, Amnon said to him, "I would like my sister Tamar to come and make some special bread in my sight, so I may eat from her hand." David sent word to Tamar at the palace: "Go to the house of your brother Amnon and prepare some food for him."*
(2 Samuel 13:1–7 NIV)

Then Amnon said to Tamar, "Bring the food here into my bedroom so I may eat from your hand." And Tamar took the bread she had prepared and brought it to her brother Amnon in his bedroom. But when she took it to him to eat, he grabbed her and said, "Come to bed with me, my sister." "No, my brother!" she said to him. "Don't force me! Such a thing should not be done in Israel! Don't do this wicked thing. What about me? Where could I get rid of my disgrace? And what about you? You would be like one of the wicked fools in Israel. Please speak to the king; he will not keep me from being married to you." But he refused to listen to her, and since he was stronger than she, he raped her.
(2 Samuel 13:10–14 NIV)

> Then Amnon hated her with intense hatred. In fact, he hated her more than he had loved her. Amnon said to her, "Get up and get out!" "No!" she said to him. "Sending me away would be a greater wrong than what you have already done to me." But he refused to listen to her. He called his personal servant and said, "Get this woman out of my sight and bolt the door after her." So his servant put her out and bolted the door after her. She was wearing an ornate robe, for this was the kind of garment the virgin daughters of the king wore. (2 Samuel 13:15–18 NIV)

Sexual desire is a creation of God and a gift given by God to mankind that is actualized in the marriage relationship for procreation and pleasure between a husband and wife.

Let's listen to the apostle Paul's statements concerning sexual desire: "But if they cannot contain, let them marry: for it is better to marry than to burn" (1 Corinthians 7:9). He also said, "But and if thou marry, thou hast not sinned" (1 Corinthians 7:28). "Let every man have his own wife" (1 Corinthians 7:2). "Flee fornication" (1 Corinthians 6:18). Review the verses listed below for further clarity:

> Flee fornication. Every sin that a man doeth is without the body; but he that committeth fornication sinneth against his own body. What? know ye not that your body is the temple of the

Holy Ghost which is in you, which ye have of God, and ye are not your own? For ye are bought with a price: therefore glorify God in your body, and in your spirit, which are God's.
(1 Corinthians 6:18–20)

But and if thou marry, thou hast not sinned; and if a virgin marry, she hath not sinned. Nevertheless such shall have trouble in the flesh: but I spare you. (1 Corinthians 7:28)

The core reason that a person gets married is that he or she is in love and would like to spend the rest of his or her life with the other person. If marriage is entered based solely for sex, that marriage is destined to fail. Also, marriage should never be about secret agendas.

Now concerning the things whereof ye wrote unto me: It is good for a man not to touch a woman. Nevertheless, to avoid fornication, let every man have his own wife, and let every woman have her own husband. Let the husband render unto the wife due benevolence: and likewise also the wife unto the husband. The wife hath not power of her own body, but the husband: and likewise also the husband hath not power of his own body, but the wife.
(1 Corinthians 7:1–4)

> *But if they cannot contain, let them marry: for it is better to marry than to burn.*
> (1 Corinthians 7:9)

> *But if any man think that he behaveth him-self uncomely toward his virgin, if she pass the flower of her age, and need so require, let him do what he will, he sinneth not: let them marry.*
> (1 Corinthians 7:36)

> *Furthermore then we beseech you, brethren, and exhort you by the Lord Jesus, that as ye have received of us how ye ought to walk and to please God, so ye would abound more and more. For ye know what commandments we gave you by the Lord Jesus. For this is the will of God, even your sanctification, that ye should abstain from fornication: That every one of you should know how to possess his vessel in sanctification and honour; Not in the lust of concupiscence, even as the Gentiles which know not God: That no man go beyond and defraud his brother in any matter: because that the Lord is the avenger of all such, as we also have forewarned you and testified. For God hath not called us unto uncleanness, but unto holiness.* (1 Thessalonians 4:1–7)

The Scriptures are replete with examples of individuals and groups who have tragically abused God's gift of sexual desire.

We will explore several situations as a reminder that we are to always honor God with our bodies while at the same time respecting the bodies of others. As stated earlier, we are created in the image of God, which is spiritual. The body is given to express God's image and not to dishonor God's image.

A. Integrity toward God

God has set certain principles and guidelines in place to keep mankind from venturing into life situations that are destructive and controlling. The Scriptures speak of the heart of mankind as characteristically wicked because of choices. Also, reliance on God is the only hope from self-destruction.

> *I call heaven and earth to record this day against you, that I have set before you life and death, blessing and cursing: therefore choose life, that both thou and thy seed may live: That thou mayest love the Lord thy God, and that thou mayest obey his voice, and that thou mayest cleave unto him: for he is thy life, and the length of thy days: that thou mayest dwell in the land which the Lord sware unto thy fathers, to Abraham, to Isaac, and to Jacob, to give them.*
> (Deuteronomy 30:19–20)

> *This people draweth nigh unto me with their mouth, and honoureth me with their lips; but their heart is far from me. But in vain*

they do worship me, teaching for doctrines the commandments of men. (Matthew 15:8–9)

This book of the law shall not depart out of thy mouth; but thou shalt meditate therein day and night, that thou mayest observe to do according to all that is written therein: for then thou shalt make thy way prosperous, and then thou shalt have good success. (Joshua 1:8)

And it shall be, when he sitteth upon the throne of his kingdom, that he shall write him a copy of this law in a book out of that which is before the priests the Levites: And it shall be with him, and he shall read therein all the days of his life: that he may learn to fear the Lord his God, to keep all the words of this law and these statutes, to do them: That his heart be not lifted up above his brethren, and that he turn not aside from the commandment, to the right hand, or to the left: to the end that he may prolong his days in his kingdom, he, and his children, in the midst of Israel. (Deuteronomy 17:18–20)

The movie *Back to the Future* featured a scene in which a character received some literature that revealed the winners of sports events in the past. The character's role was to return to the past and present himself with this literature and make the necessary adjustment, from which he would become very wealthy.

Yes, this is fictional. We cannot travel to the future to take the necessary notes, then return to the past and apply what we gathered from the future in order to control our present existence.

As human beings we are constantly faced with the unknown. We do not have the ability or capacity to project ourselves into the unknown to take the necessary notes and return to the present or reality. Because God occupies the past, present, and future at the same time, it is reasonable for human beings to place their destinies under His tutelage.

> *Ye are my witnesses, saith the Lord, and my servant whom I have chosen: that ye may know and believe me, and understand that I am he: before me there was no God formed, neither shall there be after me.* (Isaiah 43:10)

> *Thus saith the Lord the King of Israel, and his redeemer the Lord of hosts; I am the first, and I am the last; and beside me there is no God.* (Isaiah 44:6)

> *John to the seven churches which are in Asia: Grace be unto you, and peace, from him which is, and which was, and which is to come; and from the seven Spirits which are before his throne.* (Revelation 1:4)

For my thoughts are not your thoughts, neither are your ways my ways, saith the Lord. For as the heavens are higher than the earth, so are my ways higher than your ways, and my thoughts than your thoughts. (Isaiah 55:8–9)

I know the thoughts that I think toward you, saith the Lord, thoughts of peace, and not of evil, to give you an expected end. Then shall ye call upon me, and ye shall go and pray unto me, and I will hearken unto you. And ye shall seek me, and find me, when ye shall search for me with all your heart. (Jeremiah 29:11–13)

The heart is deceitful above all things, and desperately wicked: who can know it? I the Lord search the heart, I try the reins, even to give every man according to his ways, and according to the fruit of his doings. (Jeremiah 17:9–10)

Thou shalt not covet thy neighbour's house, thou shalt not covet thy neighbour's wife, nor his manservant, nor his maidservant, nor his ox, nor his ass, nor any thing that is thy neighbour's. (Exodus 20:17)

For the commandment is a lamp; and the law is light; and reproofs of instruction are the way of life: To keep thee from the evil woman, from the

flattery of the tongue of a strange woman. Lust not after her beauty in thine heart; neither let her take thee with her eyelids. For by means of a whorish woman a man is brought to a piece of bread: and the adultress will hunt for the precious life. Can a man take fire in his bosom, and his clothes not be burned? Can one go upon hot coals, and his feet not be burned? So he that goeth in to his neighbour's wife; whosoever toucheth her shall not be innocent.
(Proverbs 6:23–29)

But whoso committeth adultery with a woman lacketh understanding: he that doeth it destroyeth his own soul. A wound and dishonour shall he get; and his reproach shall not be wiped away.
(Proverbs 6:32–33)

Ye have heard that it was said by them of old time, Thou shalt not commit adultery: But I say unto you, That whosoever looketh on a woman to lust after her hath committed adultery with her already in his heart. (Matthew 5:27–28)

B. Integrity toward one's wife

For the most part, a woman would like to know that she is the only woman her husband wants as his life partner. Also, she never wants to feel that she is in competition for her husband's attention. Integrity towards one's wife is summed up in this phrase: "I'm all in." Below are some scriptures that reinforce integrity toward one's wife.

> *Live joyfully with the wife whom thou lovest all the days of the life of thy vanity, which he hath given thee under the sun, all the days of thy vanity: for that is thy portion in this life, and in thy labour which thou takest under the sun.*
> (Ecclesiastes 9:9)

> *Drink waters out of thine own cistern, and running waters out of thine own well. Let thy fountains be dispersed abroad, and rivers of waters in the streets. Let them be only thine own, and not strangers' with thee. Let thy fountain be blessed: and rejoice with the wife of thy youth. Let her be as the loving hind and pleasant roe; let her breasts satisfy thee at all times; and be thou ravished always with her love. And why wilt thou, my son, be ravished with a strange woman, and embrace the bosom of a stranger?*
> (Proverbs 5:15–20)

I am reminded of a situation that happened many years ago in which a young man was driving home one night and noticed a woman hitchhiking. He pulled over to give her a ride. She approached the car and told the driver her destination. En route the woman reached over and touched him inappropriately.

Instead of applying options to get out of this situation, he embraced it. He found a secluded spot and became physically intimate with the woman and then dropped the woman off at her destination. During that week he became physically intimate with his wife.

The wife soon began experiencing some female personal problems and made an appointment with her gynecologist. She was diagnosed as having contracted a sexually transmitted disease. Knowing that she had been intimate only with her husband, she began questioning the source of the disease. Upon confronting her husband, she discovered that he was the source of her STD because he was now being treated as well.

Now she knew where she had contracted the disease, and her husband knew where he had contracted the disease. The question that was never answered was "Where did the other woman contract the disease?" To make matters worse, the wife became pregnant, and upon delivery of the baby it was discovered that the child had this infection also. The only safe sex is no sex or sex with one's spouse exclusively.

> *And this have ye done again, covering the altar of the Lord with tears, with weeping, and with crying out, insomuch that he regardeth not the offering any more, or receiveth it with good will at your hand. Yet ye say, Wherefore? Because the Lord hath been witness between thee and the wife of thy youth, against whom thou hast dealt treacherously: yet is she thy companion,*

and the wife of thy covenant. And did not he make one? Yet had he the residue of the spirit. And wherefore one? That he might seek a godly seed. Therefore take heed to your spirit, and let none deal treacherously against the wife of his youth. (Malachi 2:13–15)

Nevertheless, to avoid fornication, let every man have his own wife, and let every woman have her own husband. Let the husband render unto the wife due benevolence: and likewise also the wife unto the husband. The wife hath not power of her own body, but the husband: and likewise also the husband hath not power of his own body, but the wife. Defraud ye not one the other, except it be with consent for a time, that ye may give yourselves to fasting and prayer; and come together again, that Satan tempt you not for your incontinency. (1 Corinthians 7:2–5)

Husbands, love your wives, even as Christ also loved the church, and gave himself for it; That he might sanctify and cleanse it with the washing of water by the word, That he might present it to himself a glorious church, not having spot, or wrinkle, or any such thing; but that it should be holy and without blemish. So ought men to love their wives as their own bodies. He that loveth his wife loveth himself. For no man ever

yet hated his own flesh; but nourisheth and cherisheth it, even as the Lord the church: For we are members of his body, of his flesh, and of his bones. For this cause shall a man leave his father and mother, and shall be joined unto his wife, and they two shall be one flesh. This is a great mystery: but I speak concerning Christ and the church. Nevertheless let every one of you in particular so love his wife even as himself; and the wife see that she reverence her husband.
(Ephesians 5:25–33)

Husbands, love your wives, and be not bitter against them. (Colossians 3:19)

Marriage is honourable in all, and the bed undefiled: but whoremongers and adulterers God will judge. (Hebrews 13:4)

Therefore shall a man leave his father and his mother and shall cleave unto his wife: and they shall be one flesh. (Genesis 2:24)

C. Integrity toward one's husband

It can be said that a man would like his wife to appreciate the strength, care, provision, protection, understanding, and compassion that he demonstrates without having to ask for the appreciation. It lends strength to the husband and sends a signal that he is a successful husband in his wife's eyes. Below are some scriptures that will help a wife demonstrate integrity toward her husband.

> *Whoso findeth a wife findeth a good thing, and obtaineth favour of the Lord.* (Proverbs 18:22)

Because the wife has been found, there is an immeasurable amount of consideration, kindness, approval, and blessing that will be unleased on her husband of which she will be the direct beneficiary. I generally tell the husband or husband-to-be that any of his achievements after marriage are because God is reaching through his wife to grant him favor. I also stress that he should let his wife know that she is the reason for his success.

> *Nevertheless, to avoid fornication, let every man have his own wife, and let every woman have her own husband.* (1 Corinthians 7:2)

> *A foolish son is the calamity of his father: and the contentions of a wife are a continual dropping. House and riches are the inheritance of fathers: and a prudent wife is from the Lord.*
> (Proverbs 19:13–14)

> *Who can find a virtuous woman? for her price is far above rubies* [she knows her value]. *The heart of her husband doth safely trust in her,*

so that he shall have no need of spoil [she is faithful]. *She will do him good and not evil all the days of her life* [she is committed]. *She seeketh wool, and flax, and worketh willingly with her hands* [she has initiative]. *She is like the merchants' ships; she bringeth her food from afar* [she is adventurous]. *She riseth also while it is yet night, and giveth meat to her household, and a portion to her maidens* [she is not lazy]. *She considereth a field, and buyeth it: with the fruit of her hands she planteth a vineyard* [she is business minded]. *She girdeth her loins with strength, and strengtheneth her arms* [she is in good physical shape]. *She perceiveth that her merchandise is good: her candle goeth not out by night* [she has a good eye for quality; she has good stamina]. *She layeth her hands to the spindle, and her hands hold the distaff* [she is a hard worker]. *She stretcheth out her hand to the poor; yea, she reacheth forth her hands to the needy* [she is generous]. *She is not afraid of the snow for her household: for all her household are clothed with scarlet* [she is not intimidated by inclement weather]. *She maketh herself coverings of tapestry; her clothing is silk and purple* [she purchases high-quality items]. *Her husband is known in the gates, when he sitteth among the elders of the land* [she brings honor to her husband]. *She maketh fine linen, and selleth it; and delivereth girdles unto the merchant* [she has a production and distribution company]. *Strength and honour are her clothing; and she shall rejoice in time to come* [she is a woman of integrity]. *She openeth her mouth with wisdom; and in her tongue is the law of kindness* [she is an educated and gentle woman]. *She looketh well to the ways of her household, and eateth not the bread of idleness* [she is serious about family and is purpose driven]. *Her children arise up, and call her blessed; her husband also, and he praiseth her* [she is well respected by her family]. *Many daughters have done virtuously, but thou excellest them all* [she is a pace-setter]. *Favour is deceitful, and beauty is vain: but a woman that feareth the Lord, she shall be praised* [she has strong inner qualities]. *Give her of the fruit of her hands; and let her own works praise her.* (Proverbs 31:10–31)

Every good gift and every perfect gift is from above, and cometh down from the Father of lights, with whom is no variableness, neither shadow of turning. (James 1:17)

The wife hath not power of her own body, but the husband: and likewise also the husband hath not power of his own body, but the wife.
(1 Corinthians 7:4)

> *Submitting yourselves one to another in the fear of God.* (Ephesians 5:21)

Many men and woman think that the only submission in a marriage relationship is to be exhibited by the wife. As in the church there is dual submission. As noted earlier, marriage is not a prison system in which there is a warden and incarceration. For a marriage to be successful there must of necessity be submission of both parties.

> *Wives, submit yourselves unto your own husbands, as unto the Lord.* (Ephesians 5:22)

The definition of *submit* is "to yield to governance or authority." The submission of a wife must be based on willingness, not fear or force. As long as a man is acting, leading, and functioning as an ambassador of the Lord Jesus Christ, a woman should be in submission. Jesus told His disciples to follow Him. Paul said to follow him as he follows Christ.

A husband should say to his wife, "Follow me as I follow Christ." If this condition is not honored by the husband, the wife will have great difficulty in submitting to her husband.

Scriptural submission has reverence for God as its foundation. When I speak of reverence, I am referring to the highest level of respect exemplified via obedience. God must be recognized as the author, sustainer, and final reality of the marriage relationship--that is, ethics, morality, fidelity, commitment, and a healthy appreciation for what is right and what is wrong. If a husband is leading in the fear or reverence of God, this provides a bridge for the wife to cross in submission, as noted earlier.

> *Therefore as the church is subject unto Christ, so let the wives be to their own husbands in everything. Husbands, love your wives, even as Christ also loved the church, and gave himself for it.* (Ephesians 5:24–25)
>
> *Husbands love your wives, and be not bitter against them.* (Colossians 3:19)
>
> *And he said to them all, If any man will come after me, let him deny himself, and take up his cross daily, and follow me.* (Luke 9:23)
>
> *Be ye followers of me, even as I also am of Christ.* (1 Corinthians 11:1)

As stated earlier, the wife being submissive to her husband doesn't mean that she is incapable of achieving an objective but is simply a matter of functionality. The success of this functionality is contingent upon the sincere demonstration of love by the husband. In short, if the husband loves his wife right, she will submit right.

Nevertheless let every one of you in particular so love his wife even as himself; and the wife see that she reverence her husband.
(Ephesians 5:33)

8

Understanding the Purpose and Power of Men

Marital Concepts, adapted from Myles Monroe

The woman is not just someone who helps here and there while the man does the real work. *Meet* actually means "fit," which means "suitable or comparable." The female is a perfect match for males in fulfilling God's purpose.

- Everything in the female is designed to help. Some men do not want the women to know that he needs her help.

- Some men see themselves as the final authorities in their homes. They don't realize that their wives are there to help them fulfill their purpose.

- Some men think that a woman was placed on earth to destroy them.

- Some men view a woman's help as a threat.

- When a woman wants to be involved in what a man is doing, he thinks she is interfering.

- A woman is the way she is because that is the way she was created.

- She wants to know what is going on so she can help (right or wrong).

- Some men can't handle the presence of a real woman.

- It takes a strong man to handle the weight of a real woman. Some men these days are even gravitating to dolls.

- God's intention for the male and female is that together their individual strengths would combine to produce exponential results.

- In his temptation the devil suggested to Adam and Eve an alternate purpose for their lives than God had already given them. They would know good and evil and supposedly become equal with God.

- In actuality, they were already like God in nature. They were created in His image and reflected His glory.

- As for knowing good and evil, there were certain things God knew it was best for them *not* to know or else He would have told them.

- God held each of them accountable because both were spiritual beings responsible to Him.

- After the fall, both the man and the woman were still responsible for ruling, but their relationship would be distorted. Instead of equality there would be imbalance.

- The woman had a longing for her husband that became controlling because that longing never seemed to be fulfilled.

- Man's twisted perception of life would cause him to want to dominate the woman, and because of sin the woman would continually desire to do anything to keep him.

9

General Scriptural Concepts Concerning Sexual Relations that Violate God's Sexual Principles and Consequences

1. Sexual violation will cause a person to turn from worshiping and serving God. Also, it is a punishable infraction before God.

> Now Israel remained in Acacia Grove, and the people began to commit harlotry with the women of Moab. They invited the people to the sacrifices of their gods, and the people ate and bowed down to their gods. So Israel was joined to Baal of Peor, and the anger of the Lord was aroused against Israel.
> (Numbers 25:1–3 NKJV)

> But Moses was furious with all the generals and captains who had returned from the battle. "Why have you let all the women live?" he demanded. "These are the very ones who

followed Balaam's advice and caused the people of Israel to rebel against the Lord at Mount Peor. They are the ones who caused the plague to strike the Lord's people. So kill all the boys and all the women who have had intercourse with a man. Only the young girls who are virgins may live; you may keep them for yourselves."
(Numbers 31:14–18 NLT)

2. Sexual violation will cause a person to lose his or her leadership position.

But king Solomon loved many strange women, together with the daughter of Pharaoh, women of the Moabites, Ammonites, Edomites, Zidonians, and Hittites: Of the nations concerning which the Lord said unto the children of Israel, Ye shall not go in to them, neither shall they come in unto you: for surely they will turn away your heart after their gods: Solomon clave unto these in love. And he had seven hundred wives, princesses, and three hundred concubines: and his wives turned away his heart. For it came to pass, when Solomon was old, that his wives turned away his heart after other gods: and his heart was not perfect with the Lord his God, as was the heart of David his father. For Solomon went after Ashtoreth the goddess of the Zidonians, and after Milcom the abomination of the Ammonites. And

Solomon did evil in the sight of the Lord, and went not fully after the Lord, as did David his father. Then did Solomon build an high place for Chemosh, the abomination of Moab, in the hill that is before Jerusalem, and for Molech, the abomination of the children of Ammon. And likewise did he for all his strange wives, which burnt incense and sacrificed unto their gods.
(1 Kings 11:1–8)

And the Lord was angry with Solomon, because his heart was turned from the Lord God of Israel, which had appeared unto him twice, And had commanded him concerning this thing, that he should not go after other gods: but he kept not that which the Lord commanded. Wherefore the Lord said unto Solomon, Forasmuch as this is done of thee, and thou hast not kept my covenant and my statutes, which I have commanded thee, I will surely rend the kingdom from thee, and will give it to thy servant.
(1 Kings 11:9–11)

3. Sexual violation will cause a person to lose his or her blessing.

"Then you added lustful Egypt to your lovers, provoking my anger with your increasing promiscuity. That is why I struck you with my fist

and reduced your boundaries. I handed you over to your enemies, the Philistines, and even they were shocked by your lewd conduct. You have prostituted yourself with the Assyrians, too. It seems you can never find enough new lovers! And after your prostitution there, you still were not satisfied. You added to your lovers by embracing Babylonia, the land of merchants, but you still weren't satisfied. What a sick heart you have, says the Sovereign Lord, to do such things as these, acting like a shameless prostitute. You build your pagan shrines on every street corner and your altars to idols in every square. In fact, you have been worse than a prostitute, so eager for sin that you have not even demanded payment. Yes, you are an adulterous wife who takes in strangers instead of her own husband. Prostitutes charge for their services—but not you! You give gifts to your lovers, bribing them to come and have sex with you. So you are the opposite of other prostitutes. You pay your lovers instead of their paying you." (Ezekiel 16:26–34 NLT)

4. Sexual violation will cause a person to destroy his or her soul and reveal his or her ignorance.

For by means of a whorish woman a man is brought to a piece of bread: and the adultress will hunt for the precious life. Can a man take fire in his bosom, and his clothes not be burned? Can one go upon hot coals, and his feet not be burned? So he that goeth in to his neighbour's wife; whosoever toucheth her shall not be innocent. (Proverbs 6:26–29)

But whoso committeth adultery with a woman lacketh understanding: he that doeth it destroyeth his own soul. A wound and dishonour shall he get; and his reproach shall not be wiped away. For jealousy is the rage of a man: therefore he will not spare in the day of vengeance. He will not regard any ransom; neither will he rest content, though thou givest many gifts.
(Proverbs 6:32–35)

5. Sexual violation can cause you to commit premeditated murder.

And it came to pass in an eveningtide, that David arose from off his bed, and walked upon the roof of the king's house: and from the roof he saw a woman washing herself; and the woman was very beautiful to look upon. And David sent and enquired after the woman. And one said, Is not this Bathsheba, the daughter of Eliam, the wife of Uriah the Hittite? And David sent messengers, and took her; and she came in unto him, and he lay with her; for she was purified

from her uncleanness: and she returned unto her house. And the woman conceived, and sent and told David, and said, I am with child.
(2 Samuel 11:2–5)

And it came to pass in the morning, that David wrote a letter to Joab, and sent it by the hand of Uriah. And he wrote in the letter, saying, Set ye Uriah in the forefront of the hottest battle, and retire ye from him, that he may be smitten, and die. And it came to pass, when Joab observed the city, that he assigned Uriah unto a place where he knew that valiant men were. And the men of the city went out, and fought with Joab: and there fell some of the people of the servants of David; and Uriah the Hittite died also.
(2 Samuel 11:14–17)

10

The Power of a Woman's Influence

Influence: the act or power of producing an effect without apparent exertion of force or direct exercise of command

Advice: guidance or recommendations concerning prudent future action, typically given by someone regarded as knowledgeable or authoritative

1. Eve

> *And when the woman saw that the tree was good for food, and that it was pleasant to the eyes, and a tree to be desired to make one wise, she took of the fruit thereof, and did eat, and gave also unto her husband with her; and he did eat.*
> (Genesis 3:6)

The extrapolation of this verse shows the power of influence. Adam had settled in his mind that he was not going to initiate eating from the tree in the middle of the garden. The influence of Eve and the fact the Adam wanted to please his wife was such that he ate fruit from the forbidden tree. It is worthy to note that there is no record of Adam or Eve disobeying God when they were single. They disobeyed God while married. The reality is that married people cover, support, and defend each other even if a wrong has been done. This is a very dangerous journey if the action of one or both spouses is negative. To enable a person in a negative activity is not unconditional love but rather supportive.

It is this type of thinking that will undermine, break down, and eventually destroy the marriage relationship. Below is another example of supportive concealment by a married couple.

2. Sarai

> *Now Sarai Abram's wife bare him no children: and she had an handmaid, an Egyptian, whose name was Hagar. And Sarai said unto Abram, Behold now, the Lord hath restrained me from bearing: I pray thee, go in unto my maid; it may be that I may obtain children by her. And Abram hearkened to the voice of Sarai. And Sarai Abram's wife took Hagar her maid the Egyptian, after Abram had dwelt ten years in the land of Canaan, and gave her to her husband Abram to be his wife. And he went in unto Hagar, and she conceived: and when she saw that she had conceived, her mistress was despised in her eyes.*
> (Genesis 16:1–4)

It is true that Abram could have easily said no based on the promise that God gave him in Genesis 15:3–4. Sarai blamed God for not allowing her to have children. Sarai gave in to the personal pressure that she was experiencing and used her *influence* to convince Abram to have sexual relationship with Hagar, her Egyptian maid.

> *And Abram said, Behold, to me thou hast given no seed: and, lo, one born in my house is mine heir. And, behold, the word of the Lord came unto him, saying, This shall not be thine heir; but he that shall come forth out of thine own bowels shall be thine heir.* (Genesis 15:3–4)

The devastating effect of Sarai's influence on Abram was her feelings of deep regret.

> *So Abram had sexual relations with Hagar, and she became pregnant. But when Hagar knew she was pregnant, she began to treat her mistress, Sarai, with contempt. Then Sarai said to Abram, "This is all your fault! I put my servant into your arms, but now that she's pregnant she treats me with contempt. The Lord will show who's wrong—you or me!" Abram replied, "Look, she is your servant, so deal with her as you see fit." Then Sarai treated Hagar so harshly that she finally ran away.* (Genesis 16:4–6 NLT)

A wife must remember that her husband has an affinity or predisposition to please his wife; that is, a husband will do whatever is in his ability to assure that she is happy.

A wife must be careful about how she leverages her influence. Pressing an issue without due consideration can and will place undue stress on the marriage relationship. Also, it will cause uncertainty on the part of the husband and a need for him to press harder to secure a remedy for his wife's happiness.

Scottish novelist George MacDonald was right when he said, "In whatever man does without God, he must fail miserably or succeed more miserably."

3. Manoah's wife

> *As the flame blazed up from the altar toward heaven, the angel of the Lord ascended in the flame. Seeing this, Manoah and his wife fell with their faces to the ground. When the angel of the Lord did not show himself again to Manoah and his wife, Manoah realized that it was the angel of the Lord. "We are doomed to die!" he said to his wife. "We have seen God!" But his wife answered, "If the Lord had meant to kill us, he would not have accepted a burnt offering and grain offering from our hands, nor shown us all these things or now told us this." The woman gave birth to a boy and named him Samson. He grew and the Lord blessed him.*
> (Judges 13:20–24 NIV)

Manoah was fixated. *Fixated* means "focusing one's attention; being stationary or unchanging." He understood from his spiritual training that to see God or a representation of God meant certain death.

The thought comes from the encounter of Moses with God. Moses wanted to see God in all his glory. God told him that it would be certain death if this occurred. So God made provision for Moses to see Him indirectly. As He passed by Moses, He placed his hand over Moses' face, shielding him from direct contact with His full glory. After passing by Moses, He removed His hand and Moses saw God's back. Note the Scripture references below.

> *And the Lord said unto Moses, I will do this thing also that thou hast spoken: for thou hast found grace in my sight, and I know thee by name. And he said, I beseech thee, shew me thy glory. And he said, I will make all my goodness pass before thee, and I will proclaim the name of the Lord before thee; and will be gracious to whom I will be gracious, and will shew mercy on whom I will shew mercy. And he said, Thou canst not see my face: for there shall no man see me, and live. And the Lord said, Behold, there is a place by me, and thou shalt stand upon a rock: And it shall come to pass, while my glory passeth by, that I will put thee in a clift of the rock, and*

will cover thee with my hand while I pass by: And I will take away mine hand, and thou shalt see my back parts: but my face shall not be seen. (Exodus 33:17–23)

"To keep your marriage brimming with love, whenever you're wrong admit it. Whenever you're right shut up" (Ogden Nash).

4. Abigail

Then Abigail made haste, and took two hundred loaves, and two bottles of wine, and five sheep ready dressed, and five measures of parched corn, and an hundred clusters of raisins, and two hundred cakes of figs, and laid them on asses. And she said unto her servants, Go on before me; behold, I come after you. But she told not her husband Nabal. And it was so, as she rode on the ass, that she came down by the covert on the hill, and, behold, David and his men came down against her; and she met them. Now David had said, Surely in vain have I kept all that this fellow hath in the wilderness, so that nothing was missed of all that pertained unto him: and he hath requited me evil for good.
(1 Samuel 25:18–21)

> *And David said to Abigail, Blessed be the Lord God of Israel, which sent thee this day to meet me: And blessed be thy advice, and blessed be thou, which hast kept me this day from coming to shed blood, and from avenging myself with mine own hand. For in very deed, as the Lord God of Israel liveth, which hath kept me back from hurting thee, except thou hadst hasted and come to meet me, surely there had not been left unto Nabal by the morning light any that pisseth against the wall. So David received of her hand that which she had brought him, and said unto her, Go up in peace to thine house; see, I have hearkened to thy voice, and have accepted thy person.* (1 Samuel 25:32–35)

Many men rob themselves of sound, beneficial, and simply practical advice because its source is female. I have heard married men say, "My wife nags, pesters, aggravates, and nearly drives me insane with her constant opinions."

During counseling sessions I have discovered that men are hearing *female,* that is, their wives, but are running it through a male filter or those things that are commonly associated with men. When David approached Abigail, his thought processes were being filtered through his mannishness. He had the skill, experience, weaponry, strength, and will to fulfill his desire on Nabal, by whom he felt insulted.

In all his destructive might, David was confronted by a woman, who presented to him and his men food, wine, and advice, of which he said was blessed. Many times a wife is trying to give her husband advice not to suppress, dominate, or disrespect but to help bring clarity and perspective to a given situation. It would be very unfortunate for a wife to have the light yet allow her husband to struggle to find his way in the dark. Because of the strong love a wife has for her husband, she will, even under opposition, light the way for her husband.

Abigail presents several ways to help a man who has a single focus but is open to advice.

1. She recognized that David had a need.
2. She recognized David's authority.
3. She recognized the need to be responsible.
4. She recognized the source of the problem.
5. She recognized that only God could stop David.
6. She recognized David's purpose.
7. She recognized her position and asked to be remembered.

5. Delilah

And she said unto him, How canst thou say, I love thee, when thine heart is not with me? thou hast mocked me these three times, and hast not told me wherein thy great strength lieth. And it came to pass, when she pressed him daily with her words, and urged him, so that his soul was vexed unto death; That he told her all his heart, and said unto her, There hath not come a razor upon mine head; for I have been a Nazarite unto God from my mother's womb: if I be shaven, then my strength will go from me, and I shall become weak, and be like any other man. And when Delilah saw that he had told her all his heart, she sent and called for the lords of the Philistines, saying, Come up this once, for he hath shewed me all his heart. Then the lords of the Philistines came up unto her, and brought money in their hand. And she made him sleep upon her knees; and she called for a man, and she caused him to shave off the seven locks of his head; and she began to afflict him, and his strength went from him. And she said, The Philistines be upon thee, Samson. And he awoke out of his sleep, and said, I will go out as at other times before, and shake myself. And he wist not that the Lord was departed from him. (Judges 16:15–20)

6. Deborah

And Deborah, a prophetess, the wife of Lapidoth, she judged Israel at that time. And she dwelt under the palm tree of Deborah between Ramah and Bethel in mount Ephraim: and the children of Israel came up to her for judgment. (Judges 4:4–5)

7. Solomon's Wives

For it came to pass, when Solomon was old, that his wives turned away his heart after other gods: and his heart was not perfect with the Lord his God, as was the heart of David his father. For Solomon went after Ashtoreth the goddess of the Zidonians, and after Milcom the abomination of the Ammonites. And Solomon did evil in the sight of the Lord, and went not fully after the Lord, as did David his father.
(1 Kings 11:4–6)

And the Lord was angry with Solomon, because his heart was turned from the Lord God of Israel, which had appeared unto him twice, And had commanded him concerning this thing, that he should not go after other gods: but he kept not that which the Lord commanded. Wherefore the Lord said unto Solomon, Forasmuch as this is done of thee, and thou hast not kept my covenant and my statutes, which I have commanded thee, I will surely rend the kingdom from thee, and will give it to thy servant. (1 Kings 11:9–11)

8. Lois and Eunice

I am reminded of your sincere faith, which first lived in your grandmother Lois and in your mother Eunice and, I am persuaded, now lives in you also. (2 Timothy 1:5 NIV)

11

Personal Relationship Traits

A *relationship* is the way two or more people, truths, or items are connected to each other. A relationship is based on acceptance, cooperation, mutual respect, and shared responsibility.

1. RELATIONSHIP—
seen in Jesus' invitation to Zacchaeus

A relationship must be active spiritually, physically, emotionally, mutually, and intellectually. A one-dimensional relationship and a non-dialogue approach between two people will eventually implode.

A key to relationship is contact and interaction. Jesus went to Zacchaeus's house. His purpose was to be in a non-interruptive dynamic where mutuality and feelings could be expressed.

When a spouse refuses to understand the principle of presence, contact, and dialogue, especially over a long period, the marriage relationship will be in crisis. It is imperative for both spouses to take this kind of behavior seriously and implement immediate steps to reverse this behavior.

> *And when Jesus came to the place, he looked up, and saw him, and said unto him, Zacchaeus, make haste, and come down; for to day I must abide at thy house. And he made haste, and came down, and received him joyfully.* (Luke 19:5–6)

2. SOCIABILITY—
seen in Jesus' dining with Matthew

It has been stated that "no man is an island." To be able to interact with other people in a mature, engaging manner typifies good social skills. In many cases parity, atmosphere, and subject will open a person up for social interaction. Being shy and introverted are recognizable social hindrances that must be addressed for sociability to take place.

Quality time—being all there

The tough part about a marriage relationship is the inevitability of becoming familiar with each other.

Ingrained in the principle of familiarity is taking the other person for granted while assuming that the spouse will condone any treatment or mistreatment without engaging in a respectful dialogue. When we conclude that our spouse doesn't need or deserve our full and loving consideration, sociability dies.

And as he passed by, he saw Levi the son of Alphaeus sitting at the receipt of custom, and said unto him, Follow me. And he arose and followed him. And it came to pass, that, as Jesus sat at meat in his house, many publicans and sinners sat also together with Jesus and his disciples: for there were many, and they followed him.
(Luke 2:14–15)

3. COMPASSION—
seen in Jesus' healing of Peter's mother-in-law

Empathy is defined as "feeling *with* someone." Sympathy is defined as "feeling *for* someone." It is clear to me that no one can know what a person is feeling on all human levels. Being hurt is the single thread within the commonality of pain and human suffering. It has been widely stated that "hurt hurts." Regardless of a person's gender, culture, or ethnic origin, feelings for the plight that human beings struggle with deserve consideration, especially spouses. Even when the feeling aspect isn't there, for the sake of the relationship the person must do what should be done.

**When you don't have love *feel*—
you must love *do*.**

**Feelings come and go,
but a decision stands alone.**

Marriage unwraps damaged goods.

Marriage is living with someone who is broken.

An individual, of course, can display tenderness, concern, and genuineness to a person who is not connected to him or her relationally. I am fully aware that this kind of behavior can be both sincere and insincere.

My point of observation is about such demonstrations that are not directed toward the person's spouse For some uncanny reason, a person can practice good behavior toward a stranger—and struggle to do the same for his or her spouse.

As stated before, when *broken* can't be fixed—it can be loved.

> *And when Jesus was come into Peter's house, he saw his wife's mother laid, and sick of a fever. And he touched her hand, and the fever left her: and she arose, and ministered unto them.*
> (Matthew 8:14–15)

.

4. THOUGHTFULNESS—
seen in Jesus' healing of the man who had been an invalid for thirty-eight years and the subsequent controversy

Thoughtfulness means "exhibiting careful, reasonable thinking."

To open the opportunity for another person to benefit from experiences learned by another feeds the relationship for intimate sharing. To be superficial robs a relationship of meaningful care and concern.

I once saw a lady carrying a baby with a baby bag and a stroller hocked on her forearm, an early-generation lightweight model. Her husband was walking ahead of her, hurrying to get into the car. He was rushing because it was raining. I heard him said to his wife, "Hurry up!"

> *Later Jesus found him at the temple and said to him, "See, you are well again. Stop sinning or something worse may happen to you." The man went away and told the Jews that it was Jesus who had made him well.* (John 5:14-15 NIV)

5. COMMUNICATIVENESS—
seen in Jesus' conversation with the woman at the well

In most cases women communicate with other women better and more deeply than they do with men. Equally true, men communicate on a deeper level with other men than they do with women. The dilemma occurs when man-to-woman or woman-to-man communication occurs. There are times in a marriage relationship when communication breaks down to poor communication using few words.

Most men are self-talkers.

The problem with self-talking is that the other person does not have a clue as to what is going on. No spouse can read another spouse's mind.

> *When a Samaritan woman came to draw water, Jesus said to her, "Will you give me a drink?" (His disciples had gone into the town to buy food.) The Samaritan woman said to him, "You are a Jew and I am a Samaritan woman. How can you ask me for a drink?" (For Jews do not associate with Samaritans.*
> (John 4:7–9 NIV)

6. GENEROSITY IN GIVING GIFTS—
seen in Jesus' conversation with
the Samaritan woman

> *Jesus answered and said unto her, If thou knewest the gift of God, and who it is that saith to thee, Give me to drink; thou wouldest have asked of him, and he would have given thee living water. . . . But whosoever drinketh of the water that I shall give him shall never thirst; but the water that I shall give him shall be in him a well of water springing up into everlasting life.*
> (John 4:10, 14)

7. **PURPOSE** (intention/intentionality)—
seen in Jesus' discourse with Peter

Then said Jesus unto him, Put up again thy sword into his place: for all they that take the sword shall perish with the sword. Thinkest thou that I cannot now pray to my Father, and he shall presently give me more than twelve legions of angels? But how then shall the scriptures be fulfilled, that thus it must be?
(Matthew 26:52–54)

When Jesus' followers saw what was going to happen, they said, "Lord, should we strike with our swords?" (Luke 22:49 NIV)

Then Simon Peter, who had a sword, drew it and struck the high priest's servant, cutting off his right ear. (The servant's name was Malchus.) (John 18:10 NIV)

But Jesus answered, "No more of this!" And he touched the man's ear and healed him.
(Luke 22:51 NIV)

8. **TILTED TOWARD THE HURTING**—
seen in the case of two blind men

And, behold, two blind men sitting by the way side, when they heard that Jesus passed by, cried out, saying, Have mercy on us, O Lord, thou son of David. And the multitude rebuked them, because they should hold their peace: but they cried the more, saying, Have mercy on us, O Lord, thou son of David. And Jesus stood still, and called them, and said, What will ye that I shall do unto you? They say unto him, Lord, that our eyes may be opened. (Matthew 20:30–33)

9. LISTENING WITH THE HEART—

seen in the case of Syro-Phoenician woman

Jesus left that place and went to the vicinity of Tyre. He entered a house and did not want anyone to know it; yet he could not keep his presence secret. In fact, as soon as she heard about him, a woman whose little daughter was possessed by an impure spirit came and fell at his feet. The woman was a Greek, born in Syrian Phoenicia. She begged Jesus to drive the demon out of her daughter. "First let the children eat all they want," he told her, "for it is not right to take the children's bread and toss it to the dogs." "Lord," she replied, "even the dogs under the table eat the children's crumbs." Then he told her, "For such a reply, you may go; the demon has left your daughter." (Mark 7:24–29 NIV)

10. RECOGNIZING AND UNDERSTANDING PEOPLE'S STRUGGLES—
seen in the case of the spirit-possessed boy

So they brought him. When the spirit saw Jesus, it immediately threw the boy into a convulsion. He fell to the ground and rolled around, foaming at the mouth. Jesus asked the boy's father, "How long has he been like this?" "From childhood," he answered. "It has often thrown him into fire or water to kill him. But if you can do anything, take pity on us and help us." "'If you can'?" said Jesus. "Everything is possible for one who believes." Immediately the boy's father exclaimed, "I do believe; help me overcome my unbelief!" (Mark 9:20–24 NIV)

11. UNSELFISHNESS—
seen in John's gospel

I am the living bread that came down from heaven. Whoever eats this bread will live forever. This bread is my flesh, which I will give for the life of the world. (John 6:51 NIV)

Biblical definition of marriage—the state of being united to a person of the opposite sex as husband or wife in a consensual and contractual relationship recognized by law and solemnized or dignified by a marriage ceremony.

Since marriage speaks of the future and the future speaks of that which is related, we need to define the term *relate*.

The Latin term for *relate* is *relatus*. *Re* means "from" and *latus* means "past"—*from the past*. Current definitions include the idea of giving an account of or carrying back.

These definitions connect the future to the past. If people are going to be people, of necessity there must be a prototype.

Prototype is defined as "an original model on which something is patterned."

If individuals chose to pattern themselves after the wrong prototype, the end result or consequences will reflect this choice—good or bad.

Whatever happens in a world of people is the result of choice. As our choices go, so will our relationships. A marriage relationship stands or falls on choice.

The common claim "I'm not hurting anyone" is usually untrue. Whether we like it or not, our actions are like ripples in a pond. A ripple is a series of small waves.

Equally so, when a line of individual dominoes is vertically positioned and the lead domino falls onto the adjacent one, the action continues until all dominoes in line fall. The initiator of the falling dominos is choice and that choice affects each succeeding domino.

We can conclude that the effect of our actions good or bad will produce an effect on another person, object, or situation. Relationships in many cases are results of observed behavior. In short, we do what we see others do.

A personal relationship is a relationship between two people who have both matured sufficiently to be capable of independence, in the sense of not becoming a prey to deep anxiety (uneasiness of mind; fearful concern) if they have to stand alone and rely on themselves.

Each person in the relationship will have developed a definite and positive personality of his or her own with the riches of stored experience and real interest. They have therefore something to give and are not in a chronic state of neediness with compulsive "getting" cravings.

They are able to appreciate each other's real and valuable qualities and can both give and receive easily and without anxiety.

Their relationship will mutually enrich them and in it they will each retain the freedom and independence of their own integrity and worth as individuals. If they are a married couple, their sexual relationship will be a spontaneous expression of their mutual desire for each other.

The ideal marriage relationship is an example of the nature of a loving, caring, and compassionate God. When individuals observe a married couple, they should be able to see clearly the characteristics of God's love for people.

Here are three thoughts from Fawn Weaver:

> *"If you're not happy with where you are and what you've got, you won't be happy with where you go or what you get. Happiness is choice for today."*

"*A great marriage is not something that just happens; it must be created.*"

"*Show me a man who is smiling from ear to ear and living a beautiful life, and I'll show you a man who is grateful for what he has and utterly in love with his wife.*"

12

Don't Tell on Me and I Won't Tell on You

It is very true that a married couple's relationship intimacy is private. Also, that which takes place in the home or behind closed doors is no one else's business. This closed-door thinking is breached when activities within the home cross moral or ethical lines. When this happens, the welfare of another is impaired, weakened, and damaged. Yes, your business is your business until it becomes someone *else's* business.

> But a certain man named Ananias, with Sapphira his wife, sold a possession, And kept back part of the price, his wife also being privy to it, and brought a certain part, and laid it at the apostles' feet. But Peter said, Ananias, why hath Satan filled thine heart to lie to the Holy Ghost, and to keep back part of the price of the land? Whiles it remained, was it not thine own? and after it was sold, was it not in thine own

> *power? why hast thou conceived this thing in thine heart? thou hast not lied unto men, but unto God. And Ananias hearing these words fell down, and gave up the ghost: and great fear came on all them that heard these things. And the young men arose, wound him up, and carried him out, and buried him. And it was about the space of three hours after, when his wife, not knowing what was done, came in. And Peter answered unto her, Tell me whether ye sold the land for so much? And she said, Yea, for so much. Then Peter said unto her, How is it that ye have agreed together to tempt the Spirit of the Lord? behold, the feet of them which have buried thy husband are at the door, and shall carry thee out. Then fell she down straightway at his feet, and yielded up the ghost: and the young men came in, and found her dead, and, carrying her forth, buried her by her husband.* (Acts 5:1–10)

Whenever the feelings of shame and guilt enter a marriage relationship, it stifles those emotions that accompany healthy relationships. Adam and Eve displayed the outward signs of a relationship that was spiraling downward. Note the conscious efforts of concealing themselves. At this point there was no openness or positive feelings.

From my experience of counseling over forty years, I have noticed an alarming depth of secrecy among spouses. When the door of communication intimacy is closed, each spouse is left imaging what messages are swirling in the other spouse's mind or what is being hidden. Again, this kind of unhealthy relationship places undue stress on the overall intimacy of the marriage and is characterized by a journey of suspicious questions and evasive answers.

> *Then the eyes of both of them were opened, and they knew that they were naked; and they sewed fig leaves together and made themselves coverings. And they heard the sound of the Lord God walking in the garden in the cool of the day, and Adam and his wife hid themselves from the presence of the Lord God among the trees of the garden. Then the Lord God called to Adam and said to him, "Where are you?" So he said, "I heard Your voice in the garden, and I was afraid because I was naked; and I hid myself."*
> (Genesis 3:7–10 NKJV)

> *In the meantime, when an innumerable multitude of people had gathered together, so that they trampled one another, He began to say to His disciples first of all, "Beware of the leaven of the Pharisees, which is hypocrisy. For there is nothing covered that will not be revealed, nor hidden that will not be known. Therefore what ever you have spoken in the dark will be heard in the light, and*

what you have spoken in the ear in inner rooms will be proclaimed on the housetops."
(Luke 12:1–3 NKJV)

For God shall bring every work into judgment, with every secret thing, whether it be good, or whether it be evil. (Ecclesiastes 12:14)

Israel hath sinned, and they have also transgressed my covenant which I commanded them: for they have even taken of the accursed thing, and have also stolen, and dissembled also, and they have put it even among their own stuff.
(Joshua 7:11)

And Joshua said unto Achan, My son, give, I pray thee, glory to the Lord God of Israel, and make confession unto him; and tell me now what thou hast done; hide it not from me. And Achan answered Joshua, and said, Indeed I have sinned against the Lord God of Israel, and thus and thus have I done: When I saw among the spoils a goodly Babylonish garment, and two hundred shekels of silver, and a wedge of gold of fifty shekels weight, then I coveted them, and took them; and, behold, they are hid in the earth in the midst of my tent, and the silver under it.
(Joshua 7:19–21)

Below are some reasons couples agree to conceal negative behavior.

1. It's nobody's business but ours.
2. I don't want to make waves in my marriage.
3. My spouse will leave me.
4. I love my current relationship.
5. What will my children think?
6. What will the neighbors think?
7. What will my church family think?
8. What will my parents think?
9. Nothing is as bad as it seems.
10. All that matters is that we're happy.
11. If no one is getting hurt, why confront?
12. The Bible doesn't expressly say that it's wrong.

Honesty and integrity are essential for authenticity in the marriage relationship, especially if "until death do us part" is embraced. Some people view the marriage commitment as fluid. Yet the voice of marriage speaks very clearly when we listen sincerely.

13

The Voice of Marriage: Children

A. **Marriage speaks of future generations.**

It is not just procreation and having children but intentionally embracing the responsibility of whole-life training, which is systematically introducing life concepts to successfully move a child through early childhood development to adolescence.

During adolescence lessons must be added leading to adulthood. What children are inundated with during their formative years can become a life norm. An important question we must ask ourselves is "What do we want the future to look like?" Role modeling is very critical to child development because children in most cases will do what adults do and not what adults say. During my marriage counseling I always reference children. I unpack the idea that the counselee's absorption, continuance, and practice of the principles discussed will impact the future of their children and those who believe in their union.

> *And Joseph dwelt in Egypt, he, and his father's house: and Joseph lived an hundred and ten years. And Joseph saw Ephraim's children of the third generation: the children also of Machir the son of Manasseh were brought up upon Joseph's knees.* (Genesis 50:22–23)

> *After this, Job lived a hundred and forty years; he saw his children and their children to the fourth generation.* (Job 42:16 NIV)

> *Lo, children are an heritage of the Lord: and the fruit of the womb is his reward. As arrows are in the hand of a mighty man; so are children of the youth. Happy is the man that hath his quiver full of them: they shall not be ashamed, but they shall speak with the enemies in the gate.* (Psalm 127:3–5)

When God places the responsibility of caring, protecting and providing for a child, whether personally conceived or adopted, it is something that should not be taken lightly. This responsibility must be accepted wholeheartedly with the end focus of preparing a child to serve God and to be productive in society.

> *A good man leaves an inheritance for his children's children, but a sinner's wealth is stored up for the righteous.* (Proverbs 13:22 NIV)

I remember listening to a song by the Temptations, a Motown singing group, that included the words "My daddy died and all he left me was alone." It is imperative that parents impart to their children skills, concepts, principles, material items, and even wealth to give them a jump start in the rhythm of life.

To exclude oneself from the future of children, especially the biologically conceived, is not good stewardship of the human dynamic. We have the responsibility to procreate and to demonstrate human values. It is true that some couples have elected not to have children for various reasons. Nevertheless, child-rearing principles do not change.

> *Children's children are a crown to the aged, and parents are the pride of their children.*
> (Proverbs 17:6 NIV)

The family should be the most stable institution on earth. When you think about it, the womb of his or her mother is the first home of a human being. The result of providing food, housing, medical attention, counsel, discipline, friendship, and so much more is necessary for a child to be productive in life.

> *Train up a child in the way he should go: and when he is old, he will not depart from it.*
> (Proverbs 22:6)

Seeing that Abraham shall surely become a great and mighty nation, and all the nations of the earth shall be blessed in him? For I know him, that he will command his children and his household after him, and they shall keep the way of the Lord, to do justice and judgment; that the Lord may bring upon Abraham that which he hath spoken of him. (Genesis 18:18–19)

And these words, which I command thee this day, shall be in thine heart: And thou shalt teach them diligently unto thy children, and shalt talk of them when thou sittest in thine house, and when thou walkest by the way, and when thou liest down, and when thou risest up. (Deuteronomy 6:6–7)

And, ye fathers, provoke not your children to wrath: but bring them up in the nurture and admonition of the Lord. (Ephesians 6:4)

To Timothy, my dearly beloved son: Grace, mercy, and peace, from God the Father and Christ Jesus our Lord. (2 Timothy 1:2)

When I call to remembrance the unfeigned faith that is in thee, which dwelt first in thy grandmother Lois, and thy mother Eunice; and I am persuaded that in thee also. (2 Timothy 1:5)

Training a child is not a single lesson but rather an unending series of life lessons that encompass teaching by telling and doing. Children will eventually value what adults *practice* more than what they *say*.

It is obvious that humans are not perfect, yet adults must put forth the best possible example of how to engage in life scenarios. Life lessons must be taught for the sake of a child's future even though there is no guarantee that a child will follow them. Below are some scriptural examples of lessons taught but not followed or not taught at all.

> *And Nadab and Abihu, the sons of Aaron, took either of them his censer, and put fire therein, and put incense thereon, and offered strange fire before the Lord, which he commanded them not. And there went out fire from the Lord, and devoured them, and they died before the Lord.* (Leviticus 10:1–2)

> *And Elkanah went to Ramah to his house. And the child did minister unto the Lord before Eli the priest.* (1 Samuel 2:11)

> *Now Eli was very old, and heard all that his sons did unto all Israel; and how they lay with the women that assembled at the door of the tabernacle of the congregation. And he said unto them, Why do ye such things? for I hear of your evil dealings by all this people.* (1 Samuel 2:22–23)

B. **Marriage speaks of sexual purity.**

Numerous behaviors and practices taking place in our current society are eroding the purity and beauty of sexual union, which is to be actualized in the context of marriage between a man and a woman. The privacy of this relationship is now surrounded by glass walls through which anyone can participate in the intimacy of the marriage bed.

The suggestive magazine covers, the proliferation of all kinds of porn, the acceptance of same-sex relationships, various media presentations, and even bestiality (sexual relations with animals) are drowning out the voice of sexual purity to the point that sexual purity is experiencing a slow death.

Marriage is the only institution that is speaking against sexual death. Instead of a husband and wife embarking on a journey of sexual discovery, they are trying to repeat the sexual revolution practices that don't fit their willingness or skill set.

Some real-life situations have been brought to my attention in which wives are waiting somewhat impatiently in the bedroom while their husbands are looking at porn on the computer trying to get ready to be intimate with their wives. These relationships ended in divorce, the grounds being the wives' inability to compete with a computer.

The numbing of sexual shame and the lack of embarrassment and blushing seem to be the order of the day. The following scripture reveals that the Israelites had drifted so far away from God's value system that they had lost their ability to react to that which causes shame:

> *They have healed also the hurt of the daughter of my people slightly, saying, Peace, peace; when there is no peace. Were they ashamed when they had committed abomination? nay, they were not at all ashamed, neither could they blush: therefore they shall fall among them that fall: at the time that I visit them they shall be cast down, saith the Lord.* (Jeremiah 6:14–15)

Paul in writing to Timothy said that in the last days there would be a move to forbid individuals to marry (1 Timothy 4:3). The underlying principle in this forbiddance is the blatant disregard for scriptural values that surround and support the marriage relationship.

God, who is our final reality, created male and female with the ability to have sexual relationship. He also created male and female with the ability to choose commitment, fidelity, abstinence, and integrity.

This ability was not just to have children but to enjoy sexual intimacy within the context of marriage. The trouble that people run into with the sexual revolution is exposure under the banner of freedom with the absence of responsibility. In many cases the sexual exposure comes too early in a person's life, resulting in experimentation with disastrous conclusions. When mankind substitutes God's guidelines with sexual gratification, the image of God in man and the body God created are disrespected.

Knowing that the human body deteriorates over time, regardless of our efforts to slow the process, we see that the invisible qualities must be our focus to a "to death do us part" relationship. God's Word indicates that only people are created in His image. This image must be and should be a major consideration throughout the journey of a marriage relationship

> *Marriage is honourable in all, and the bed undefiled: but whoremongers and adulterers God will judge.* (Hebrews 13:4)

> *Drink water from your own cistern, running water from your own well. Should your springs overflow in the streets, your streams of water in the public squares? Let them be yours alone, never to be shared with strangers.*
> (Proverbs 5:15–17 NIV)

It is said that behavior, conduct, and actions are more caught than taught. For the most part, people are trying to discover their identities. This search in most cases is realized through observation. Even though people strive to be their own persons, humans directly and indirectly learn from each other and then choose.

A young man once said to me that he's not responsible for his sexual deviations or proclivities because it's God who gave him the desire to have sex and that he should not be scrutinized for actualizing what is natural or intrinsic.

I spoke with another young man who bragged about the number of young women that he had sex with and the number of children he produced. I looked him squarely in the face and said, "I hope that each of the women file child support against you. Maybe the reduction in your income will cause you to act responsibly."

The kind of logic displayed by these young men suggests that persons committing criminal acts should not be persecuted or restricted from fulfilling their genetic mapping, which places mankind in a mechanistic, automated realm. Based on our current social system, personal responsibility for our actions and their subsequent consequences are inescapable because it is commonly accepted that human beings can choose. One young man said that the reason he cannot keep his hands off a girl is that his hand had "a mind of its own." This kind of thinking predisposes a person to disrespect and becomes a default excuse for his or her actions.

Just because a person says that he or she is acting from an internal genetic predisposition doesn't exonerate him or her from personal liability. Each person must take responsibility and control of his or her body. This truth is verified in the scriptures below:

> *For this is the will of God, your sanctification: that you should abstain from sexual immorality; that each of you should know how to possess his own vessel in sanctification and honor, not in*

passion of lust, like the Gentiles who do not know God; that no one should take advantage of and defraud his brother in this matter, because the Lord is the avenger of all such, as we also forewarned you and testified.
(1 Thessalonians 4:3–6 NKJV)

I beseech you therefore, brethren, by the mercies of God, that you present your bodies a living sacrifice, holy, acceptable to God, which is your reasonable service. And do not be conformed to this world, but be transformed by the renewing of your mind, that you may prove what is that good and acceptable and perfect will of God.
(Romans 12:1–2 NKJV)

Do you not know that your bodies are members of Christ? Shall I then take the members of Christ and make them members of a harlot? Certainly not! Or do you not know that he who is joined to a harlot is one body with her? For "the two," He says, "shall become one flesh." But he who is joined to the Lord is one spirit with Him. Flee sexual immorality. Every sin that a man does is outside the body, but he who commits sexual immorality sins against his own body. Or do you not know that your body is the temple of the

> *Holy Spirit who is in you, whom you have from God, and you are not your own? For you were bought at a price; therefore glorify God in your body and in your spirit, which are God's.*
> (1 Corinthians 6:15–20 NKJV)

The statement "I am my own person" is validated through observing and being observed. For me to be me, I must allow you to be you. Herein is a challenge during the marriage journey. To allow one's spouse to develop, mature, and experience life within the context of the marriage relationship is accomplished successfully only within the context of love that includes personal responsibility to the relationship. Marriage embraces the principle of interdependence or that which is reciprocally carried on between two individuals.

The dilemma that some married couples wrestle with is the fact that their spouses do not act like them. This surprise comes because the dating or engagement phase of the relationship did not allow the couple to see their differences. Now in the continuance and closeness of the marriage relationship, the married couples' observation of each other becomes more microscopic than blanket acceptance.

The ability to allow a spouse the freedom to develop at his or her own pace is an act of love. I'm not saying that there should not be coercion. Yet the coercion must be gentle, mild, and full of sympathy, empathy, and with the spouse's best interests front and center.

Each spouse has a dynamic effect on the marriage relationship because his or her contribution yields both strengths and weaknesses. These attributes reside in both spouses. God's Word says that Adam was alone, that is, there was no one like him. Adam needed Eve. The same can be said of Eve. If Eve were alone, she would need someone like Adam. In the marriage dynamic no one spouse has all the faults nor does he or she have all the answers.

I am my own person.

Alfred Adler said, "What people want most of all is power." It's not the kind of power that helps another person to develop but the kind of power that dominates. Many marriage relationships fail because of the constant power struggle between spouses. No one wants to feel that he or she has no voice in a relationship. As a matter of fact, one sign of an unhealthy marriage is when one spouse is sequestered. Walter Payton said, "We are stronger together than we are apart."

The word *control* means "to guide or manage from a position of power or authority." The biblical marriage model is a shared power. Each person in the marriage relationship has not only a vested interest but also a voice that is vital to the relationship.

Marriage is a biblical covenant with a "stranger" (one not belonging to the family or household) who is capable of thought, opinion, conclusions, and so much more. To submit to a person means that due consideration will be given to that person's position to determine if it is a more suitable direction.

The biblical perspective is for the husband to love his wife *as Christ loved the church* and for the wife to reverence her husband. That is, if a husband loves his wife right, the consequence is that his wife will submit right. If a husband does not love his wife according to God's principles, she should not give up on life but use her talents and strengths to succeed in life.

Nadine and I taught our four daughters that they can take care of themselves. If they desire a husband, they are to communicate that "I want you in my life, but if that doesn't happen, I don't need you in order to *have* a life."

C. Marriage speaks of the uniqueness of love.

> *For God so loved the world, that he gave his only begotten Son, that whosoever believeth in him should not perish, but have everlasting life.*
> (John 3:16)

The word *so* means "in this way or manner." God is fully aware of mankind's ability to do the worse kind of activities. God has chosen to love us regardless of what He knows about us and what we can do.

Many couples base the success of their marriages on feelings. Also, many couples use feelings as the barometer to determine the quality and depth of their love. I fully subscribe to the fact that love has a feeling component. The reality about feelings, however, is that they come and go.

I have talked to married couples who say that they have no feelings for their spouses. My counsel is that when you do not have love feelings, you must practice love *doing* until the feelings return.

Some people think that their marriage is over because they don't feel what they felt early on in their relationship. Marriage is a decision. When God decided to love us, His decision was based not on feelings but choice. God chose to love us unconditionally. So it must be with spouses. For example, if we went to our places of employment based on day-to-day feelings, we would be in jeopardy of smaller paychecks or even being let go. We go to work because of choice, in order to enjoy the benefits that employment provides.

> *For God sent not his Son into the world to condemn the world; but that the world through him might be saved.* (John 3:17)

My wife, Nadine, said, "If you can find something wrong with someone, you can also find something right." It's all about focus. A person can focus on the negative and build a monumental case. Equally so, he or she can find something positive as steps to a greater and more endearing relationship.

Don't hurt my hurt—lean on me.

> *And Jacob was left alone; and there wrestled a man with him until the breaking of the day.*

> *And when he saw that he prevailed not against him, he touched the hollow of his thigh; and the hollow of Jacob's thigh was out of joint, as he wrestled with him. And he said, Let me go, for the day breaketh. And he said, I will not let thee go, except thou bless me.* (Genesis 32:24–26)

Jacob's wrestling left him "dis-jointed." His goal was to be blessed with a reprieve or favor from his upcoming encounter with his brother Esau. God granted him favor but he still walked with a limp, which was a reminder of his struggle.

Individual struggles vary in many respects and can be discussed on many different levels. Suffice it to say at this point that life's struggles can leave lasting scars.

I remember during the dismantling of our church garage that I leaned over to remove a dry wall screw only to fall. During the fall my arm slid across the face of the plywood and onto the drywall screw. I felt sharp pain rush through my right arm and then noticed that about a three-and-a-half-inch line of skin was removed from my forearm. The result from the healing process was something called a "keloid," a thick scar resulting from excessive growth of fibrous tissue.

I am asked from time to time about his keloid, which really looked bad shortly after the initial injury. For the most part, I am glad when I can just cover it up with a jacket or shirt. I think this is true about emotional scars as well. People find creative ways to cover them up. Yet in the marriage relationship Adam and Eve were completely exposed to each other, with nothing hidden. Concealed scars, which are reminders of struggles, will be exposed.

Marriage is the joining together of two imperfect people.

Never take any moment of your marriage relationship for granted; moments lead to hours and hours lead to days and days lead to weeks.

Love will always find its way back to arms of love.

Love: an unselfish, loyal, passionate tenderness and benevolent concern for the good of another.

Love is a decision with feeling as its generator but not its sustainer, because feelings change.

Because married couples become so familiar with each other, they can slip into what I would call a "passive neutral mind-set." Couples stop engaging because they know the response they will receive from their spouses. The anticipation of spontaneity becomes buried.

For example, a person can become so familiar with a certain food that he or she chooses not to eat it even if it is a healthful food. What has happened? The person's ability to taste is not positively challenged.

Just as with a dance partner, all the choreographed steps are so well rehearsed that the dancers will not miss a step even without the music playing. Even so, with married couples the disengagement is not because they have not chosen each other but because they are so *familiar* with each other.

To love someone is a daily choice.

Smothering vs. Space

I have fond memories of the days when wearing a seatbelt was not mandatory. In fact, many vehicles did not even have seatbelts. There were occasions when you would see a couple in the front seat of the car sitting so close together that from a distance it looked as if the only person was in the vehicle. In my thinking, smothering is when a spouse makes it very uncomfortable for the other person to relax because of exaggerated clinging.

Cuddling, hugging, embracing, and so on have their place in the marriage relationship. When they become distorted and uncomfortable for the other person, the situation must be addressed appropriately before resentment develops.

14

Love Must Be Full of Integrity

Now the serpent was more subtil than any beast of the field which the Lord God had made. And he said unto the woman, Yea, hath God said, Ye shall not eat of every tree of the garden?
(Genesis 3:1)

Regardless of the subtitles of life, spouses must maintain a high level of consciousness for the success of the marriage relationship. Whenever spouses allow themselves to reduce their biblical valves, their marriage relationship will suffer.

How do you know when the Devil is lying? Every time he talks.

And the woman said unto the serpent, We may eat of the fruit of the trees of the garden: But of the fruit of the tree which is in the midst of the garden, God hath said, Ye shall not eat of

> *it, neither shall ye touch it, lest ye die. And the serpent said unto the woman, Ye shall not surely die: For God doth know that in the day ye eat thereof, then your eyes shall be opened, and ye shall be as gods, knowing good and evil.*
> (Genesis 3:1–5)

If God wanted to, He could have made Adam and Eve robots instead of giving them the ability to choose. Imagine having a spouse who was a robot, which responded only to commands and not from initiative or consciousness. God designed human beings with the ability to communicate on a higher level, which encompasses self-awareness, choice, intention, and forethought.

Obedience is proven through testing.

It is imperative that the woman be strong in God. The tendency to lean on the husband's strength is not enough. Below is a list of women in the Bible who exemplified strength of character.

1. Ruth

> *And Naomi said, turn again, my daughters: why will ye go with me? are there yet any more sons in my womb, that they may be your husbands?* (Ruth 1:11)

And Ruth said, Intreat me not to leave thee, or to return from following after thee: for whither thou goest, I will go; and where thou lodgest, I will lodge: thy people shall be my people, and thy God my God: Where thou diest, will I die, and there will I be buried: the Lord do so to me, and more also, if ought but death part thee and me. (Ruth 1:16–17)

2. Deborah

And the children of Israel again did evil in the sight of the Lord, when Ehud was dead. And the Lord sold them into the hand of Jabin king of Canaan, that reigned in Hazor; the captain of whose host was Sisera, which dwelt in Harosheth of the Gentiles. And the children of Israel cried unto the Lord: for he had nine hundred chariots of iron; and twenty years he mightily oppressed the children of Israel. And Deborah, a prophetess, the wife of Lapidoth, she judged Israel at that time. (Judges 4:1–4)

And Barak said unto her, If thou wilt go with me, then I will go: but if thou wilt not go with me, then I will not go. And she said, I will surely go with thee: notwithstanding the journey that thou takest shall not be for thine honour; for the Lord shall sell Sisera into the hand of a woman. And Deborah arose, and went with Barak to Kedesh. (Judges 4:8–9)

3. Abigail

But one of the young men told Abigail, Nabal's wife, saying, Behold, David sent messengers out of the wilderness to salute our master; and he railed on them. But the men were very good unto us, and we were not hurt, neither missed we any thing, as long as we were conversant with them, when we were in the fields: They were a wall unto us both by night and day, all the while we were with them keeping the sheep.
(1 Samuel 25:24–16)

Now therefore know and consider what thou wilt do; for evil is determined against our master, and against all his household: for he is such a son of Belial, that a man cannot speak to him. Then Abigail made haste, and took two hundred loaves, and two bottles of wine, and five sheep ready dressed, and five measures of parched corn, and an hundred clusters of raisins, and two hundred cakes of figs, and laid them on asses. And she said unto her servants, Go on before me; behold, I come after you. But she told not her husband Nabal. (1 Samuel 25:17–19)

And it was so, as she rode on the ass, that she came down by the covert on the hill, and, behold, David and his men came down against her; and she met them. Now David had said, Surely in vain have I kept all that this fellow hath in the wilderness, so that nothing was missed of all that pertained unto him: and he hath requited me evil for good. So and more also do God unto the enemies of David, if I leave of all that pertain to him by the morning light any that pisseth against the wall. (1 Samuel 25:20–22)

And when Abigail saw David, she hasted, and lighted off the ass, and fell before David on her face, and bowed herself to the ground, And fell at his feet, and said, Upon me, my lord, upon me let this iniquity be: and let thine handmaid, I pray thee, speak in thine audience, and hear the words of thine handmaid. Let not my lord, I pray thee, regard this man of Belial, even Nabal: for as his name is, so is he; Nabal is his name, and folly is with him: but I thine handmaid saw not the young men of my lord, whom thou didst send. (1 Samuel 25:23–25)

And David said to Abigail, Blessed be the Lord God of Israel, which sent thee this day to meet me: And blessed be thy advice, and blessed be thou, which hast kept me this day from coming to shed blood, and from avenging myself with mine own hand. (1 Samuel 25:32–33)

4. Hannah

So Hannah rose up after they had eaten in Shiloh, and after they had drunk. Now Eli the priest sat upon a seat by a post of the temple of the Lord. And she was in bitterness of soul, and prayed unto the Lord, and wept sore. And she vowed a vow, and said, O Lord of hosts, if thou wilt indeed look on the affliction of thine handmaid, and remember me, and not forget thine handmaid, but wilt give unto thine handmaid a man child, then I will give him unto the Lord all the days of his life, and there shall no razor come upon his head. (1 Samuel 1:9–11)

For this child I prayed; and the Lord hath given me my petition which I asked of him: Therefore also I have lent him to the Lord; as long as he liveth he shall be lent to the Lord. And he worshipped the Lord there. (1 Samuel 1:27–28)

5. Esther

For if thou altogether holdest thy peace at this time, then shall there enlargement and deliverance arise to the Jews from another place; but thou and thy father's house shall be destroyed: and who knoweth whether thou art come to the kingdom for such a time as this? Then Esther bade them return Mordecai this answer, Go, gather together all the Jews that are present in Shushan, and fast ye for me, and neither eat nor drink three days, night or day: I also and my maidens will fast likewise; and so will I go in unto the king, which is not according to the law: and if I perish, I perish. (Esther 4:14–16)

6. Lois and Eunice

I thank God, whom I serve from my forefathers with pure conscience, that without ceasing I have remembrance of thee in my prayers night and day; Greatly desiring to see thee, being mindful of thy tears, that I may be filled with joy; When I call to remembrance the unfeigned faith that is in thee, which dwelt first in thy grandmother Lois, and thy mother Eunice; and I am persuaded that in thee also. (2 Timothy 1:3–5)

**Hurt people hurt people.
Healthy people help people.**

7. Woman with the issue of blood

And a woman having an issue of blood twelve years, which had spent all her living upon physicians, neither could be healed of any, Came behind him, and touched the border of his garment: and immediately her issue of blood stanched. And Jesus said, Who touched me? When all denied, Peter and they that were with him said, Master, the multitude throng thee and press thee, and sayest thou, Who touched me?
(Luke 8:43–45)

8. Mary, the mother of Jesus

And the angel said unto her, Fear not, Mary: for thou hast found favour with God. And, behold, thou shalt conceive in thy womb, and bring forth a son, and shalt call his name Jesus. He shall be great, and shall be called the Son of the Highest: and the Lord God shall give unto him the throne of his father David: And he shall reign over the house of Jacob for ever; and of his kingdom there shall be no end. Then said Mary unto the angel, How shall this be, seeing I know not a man? And the angel answered and said unto her, The Holy Ghost shall come upon thee, and the power of the Highest shall overshadow thee: therefore also that holy thing which shall be born of thee shall be called the Son of God.
(Luke 1:30–35)

8. Eve

And when the woman saw that the tree was good for food, and that it was pleasant to the eyes, and a tree to be desired to make one wise, she took of the fruit thereof, and did eat, and gave also unto her husband with her; and he did eat. (Genesis 3:6)

Adam and Eve disobeyed God in a marriage relationship. Every man is his own Adam and every woman is her own Eve. Because a husband and wife live together and see each other's reactions as they face the vicissitudes of life, they become very familiar with each other's short coming or weaknesses. Because the marriage relationship is personal and private, marital secrets began to develop. The sad scenario is that those secrets become marital coverups. The coverups evolve into a pretense that all is well when it is not.

James Dobson coined the well-known phrase "tough love." A husband or wife does the other a disservice by not confronting a behavior that is destructive both to the individual personally and the marital relationship. I remember a woman who was fully aware that her husband was engaged in watching porn—but because it made him happy, she did not want to confront him. Because of the nature of this behavior, she did not seek outside counsel. Eventually her husband's interest in her was all but gone. The tragedy is that the marital relationship had deteriorated beyond repair. Below are prime examples of coverups that led to pretense and deceptive practices:

But a certain man named Ananias, with Sapphira his wife, sold a possession, And kept back part of the price, his wife also being privy to it, and brought a certain part, and laid it at the apostles' feet. But Peter said, Ananias, why hath Satan filled thine heart to lie to the Holy Ghost, and to keep back part of the price of the land? Whiles it remained, was it not thine own? and after it was sold, was it not in thine own power? why hast thou conceived this thing in thine heart? thou hast not lied unto men, but unto God. And Ananias hearing these words fell down, and gave up the ghost: and great fear came on all them that heard these things. And the young men arose, wound him up, and carried him out, and buried him. And it was about the space of three hours after, when his wife, not knowing what was done, came in. And Peter answered unto her, Tell me whether ye sold the land for so much? And she said, Yea, for so much. Then Peter said unto her, How is it that ye have agreed together to tempt the Spirit of the Lord? behold, the feet of them which have buried thy husband are at the door, and shall carry thee out. Then fell she down straightway at his feet, and yielded up the ghost: and the young men came in, and found her dead, and, carrying her forth, buried her by her husband.
(Acts 5:1–10)

But the children of Israel committed a trespass in the accursed thing: for Achan, the son of Carmi, the son of Zabdi, the son of Zerah, of the tribe of Judah, took of the accursed thing: and the anger of the Lord was kindled against the children of Israel. (Joshua 7:1)

And Joshua said unto Achan, My son, give, I pray thee, glory to the Lord God of Israel, and make confession unto him; and tell me now what thou hast done; hide it not from me. And Achan answered Joshua, and said, Indeed I have sinned against the Lord God of Israel, and thus and thus have I done: When I saw among the spoils a goodly Babylonish garment, and two hundred shekels of silver, and a wedge of gold of fifty shekels weight, then I coveted them, and took them; and, behold, they are hid in the earth in the midst of my tent, and the silver under it. (Joshua 7:19–21)

And Nadab and Abihu, the sons of Aaron, took either of them his censer, and put fire therein, and put incense thereon, and offered strange fire before the Lord, which he commanded them not. And there went out fire from the Lord, and devoured them, and they died before the Lord. (Leviticus 10:1–2)

But Gehazi, the servant of Elisha the man of God, said, Behold, my master hath spared Naaman this Syrian, in not receiving at his hands that which he brought: but, as the Lord liveth, I will run after him, and take somewhat of him. So Gehazi followed after Naaman. And when Naaman saw him running after him, he lighted down from the chariot to meet him, and said, Is all well? And he said, All is well. My master hath sent me, saying, Behold, even now there be come to me from mount Ephraim two young men of the sons of the prophets: give them, I pray thee, a talent of silver, and two changes of garments.
(2 Kings 5:20–22)

And Naaman said, Be content, take two talents. And he urged him, and bound two talents of silver in two bags, with two changes of garments, and laid them upon two of his servants; and they bare them before him. And when he came to the tower, he took them from their hand, and bestowed them in the house: and he let the men go, and they departed. But he went in, and stood before his master. And Elisha said unto him, Whence comest thou, Gehazi? And he said, Thy servant went no whither.
(2 Kings 5:23–25)

The devil doesn't want you to have a good or great marriage.

"Love is a partnership of two unique people who bring out the very best in each other and who know that even though they are wonderful as individuals, they are even better together" (Barbara Cage). The sad part is that married couples can also bring out the worse in each other. That's why biblical principles coupled with an ongoing diet of reading about marriage and attending marriage seminars are extremely helpful.

> *Therefore the Lord God sent him forth from the garden of Eden, to till the ground from whence he was taken. So he drove out the man; and he placed at the east of the garden of Eden Cherubims, and a flaming sword which turned every way, to keep the way of the tree of life.* (Genesis 3:23–24)

There is a level of satisfaction that will always be just beyond our reach.

Contrary to many others, married couples are incapable of fulfilling every need of each other. That level of satisfaction can be filled only by God and God alone. This is the dilemma or hurdle that married couples sometimes fail to understand. Because of this failure, dissatisfaction, disappointment, and disfunction become the dominant emotions of the marriage relationship.

If there is no reprieve or improvement, one or both spouses will become interested in other things, if not another person. This, then, is a sure recipe for a shipwrecked marriage.

During one counselling session I told a couple that they had lost sight of a critical fact—that they had not married themselves. They were married to each other, and the other spouse was completely different from the other one physically, experientially, intellectually, and in many other ways. I did not mean for this statement to be one of defiance but a point of clarity to help resolve conflict.

A spouse will not act exactly like the other spouse. To accept this difference is the miracle of the marriage dynamic. It is perfectly within reason for a spouse to say, "I'm not you."

Individuality is not to be sacrificed in the marriage relationship.

Marriage is a matter of the *heart*, which refers to individual core values (foundational principles), the real meaning of something.

15

Unconditional Love Requires a Condition

Unconditional love has a one-directional theme that says regardless of a person's state or lot in life, love will not be withheld. Yet the individual being loved is not without reciprocal responsibility.

When thinking of the unconditional principle of love, there must not and should not be an abandonment of right living or right response. Unconditional love doesn't give a spouse license to continue to engage in bad, disruptive or destructive behavior. Rather, it leaves the door open for a spouse to come back home. Once in the home, the wayward spouse must make the necessary adjustment to remain. It is very unfair for one spouse to maintain an unconditional love interest and the other to take advantage of this. Both spouses must maintain this type of love for each other with the understanding that conditions are required for the marriage relationship to be healthy. The scriptures below reveal this concept:

When Jesus had lifted up himself, and saw none but the woman, he said unto her, Woman, where are those thine accusers? hath no man condemned thee? She said, No man, Lord. And Jesus said unto her, Neither do I condemn thee: go, and sin no more. (John 8:10–11)

And he that was healed wist not who it was: for Jesus had conveyed himself away, a multitude being in that place. Afterward Jesus findeth him in the temple, and said unto him, Behold, thou art made whole: sin no more, lest a worse thing come unto thee. The man departed, and told the Jews that it was Jesus, which had made him whole. (John 5:13–14)

Likewise, I say unto you, there is joy in the presence of the angels of God over one sinner that repenteth. (Luke 15:10)

I tell you, Nay: but, except ye repent, ye shall all likewise perish. (Luke 13:3)

Wash you, make you clean; put away the evil of your doings from before mine eyes; cease to do evil; Learn to do well; seek judgment, relieve the oppressed, judge the fatherless, plead for the widow. Come now, and let us reason together, saith the Lord: though your sins be as scarlet, they shall be as white as snow; though they be red like crimson, they shall be as wool. If ye be willing and obedient, ye shall eat the good of the land: But if ye refuse and rebel, ye shall be devoured with the sword: for the mouth of the Lord hath spoken it. (Isaiah 1:16–20)

Therefore I will judge you, O house of Israel, every one according to his ways, saith the Lord God. Repent, and turn yourselves from all your transgressions; so iniquity shall not be your ruin. Cast away from you all your transgressions, whereby ye have transgressed; and make you a new heart and a new spirit: for why will ye die, O house of Israel? For I have no pleasure in the death of him that dieth, saith the Lord God: wherefore turn yourselves, and live ye.
(Ezekiel 18:30–32)

This is a faithful saying, and worthy of all acceptation, that Christ Jesus came into the world to save sinners; of whom I am chief. Howbeit for this cause I obtained mercy, that in me first Jesus Christ might shew forth all longsuffering, for a pattern to them which should hereafter believe on him to life everlasting. (1 Timothy 1:15–16)

Love can be defined as a strong feeling for person relating to kinship or common experiences or backgrounds. It can also be defined as an unselfish, magnanimous, thoughtful concern for the good of another.

**Love is a decision with feeling
as its generator—
but not its sustainer.**

Loving someone is a daily choice.

Some say that once a person enters love, all he or she needs to do is hold on for the ride of a lifetime. This is a misdiagnosis. There is no point in the marriage relationship at which a person can ignore a conscious choice factor. Marriage demands full engagement at every point. Countless detours, attention-stealers, and interests will exert pressure to derail the marriage relationship in part if not altogether. Once my wife, Nadine, said, "I don't feel that you love me." Hearing this was very alarming, and I was at a loss for words. Finally in my male-mindedness I said, "The grass is mowed, the house is in good repair, both of our cars run, the door and window locks are operational." I noticed that my answers were not home runs. Finally I asked Nadine, "What is your definition of love?" She said, "Just to sit and talk with me, hold me for no other reason, take walks with me, and smile more." When I began implementing these fruits of love from a female perspective, Nadine then said to me, "Now I know that you love me."

Love must involve acts of kindness that focus in on a spouse's needs with no hidden agendas. Now this does not diminish the vocalization of the intimate yet sometimes abused declaration "I love you." Once during a counseling session a man said, "My wife never tells me that she loves me." The wife said, "I told you that fifteen years ago when we got married, and nothing has changed." Speaking love affirmation is a positive motivation for the person at the end of the affirmation. Both the speaking and the doing of the love principle are necessary. This concept is embodied in the scripture below.

> *My little children, let us not love in word, neither in tongue; but in deed and in truth.*
> (1 John 3:18)

The dynamic intimacy of love cannot be fully realized without both sides being engaged. There must be communication that expresses what each spouse thinks and feels toward the other.

> *For God so loved the world that he gave His only begotten Son, that whosoever believeth in him should not perish, but have everlasting life.*
> (John 3:16)

The greatest expression of love is *giving*, and love's only anticipation is that the individual will receive what is given. In many cases people entering marriage have a misguided perception concerning serving, which has its foundation in unselfishness. Some people have the mind-set that they are to be served and not serve; that is, they are very comfortable with receiving but struggle in giving or serving. If a marriage relationship is to be still vibrant and strong, there must be shared giving, serving, and receiving.

> *I have shewed you all things, how that so labouring ye ought to support the weak, and to remember the words of the Lord Jesus, how he said, It is more blessed to give than to receive.*
> (Acts 20:35)

To place one's heart in the hands of another is both dangerous and delightful.

From what I have read and experienced, some cultural groups elevate male preference. The man is to be cared for first with a blatant disregard for the woman's need for equality. Imagine the depth of appreciation that would surface if married couples genuinely served each other. Giving or serving includes time, energy, and resources within reason as spouses express respect and caring for each other. Listen to Matthew as he speaks about felt feelings in the verse below.

> *Therefore all things whatsoever ye would that men should do to you, do ye even so to them: for this is the law and the prophets.*
> (Matthew 7:12)

I'm talking about a service that is not out of duty, undue pressure, or hidden agenda—but its sole motivation is to meet the needs of another from a heart of love. The apostle Paul's declaration to the Galatians and Jesus' declaration to His disciples pronounces this principle loud and clear.

> *There is neither Jew nor Greek, there is neither bond nor free, there is neither male nor female: for ye are all one in Christ Jesus.*
> (Galatians 3:28)

> *For, brethren, ye have been called unto liberty; only use not liberty for an occasion to the flesh, but by love serve one another.*
> (Galatians 5:13)

> *Where there is neither Greek nor Jew, circumcision nor uncircumcision, Barbarian, Scythian, bond nor free: but Christ is all, and in all.* (Colossians 3:11)

> *For there is no respect of persons with God.*
> (Romans 2:11)

> *Then Peter opened his mouth, and said, Of a truth I perceive that God is no respecter of persons.* (Acts 10:34)

The lover doesn't want to hurt the object of what it loves.

You don't want to hurt the one who loves you.

It is true that unintentional situations happen in a marriage relationship that end up causing one or both spouses pain and hurt. The objective is to avoid hurting your spouse, especially hurting or causing them pain intentionally. Whenever a spouse intentionally hurts or cause pain, real or imagined, it will reduce the effectiveness of the one being hurt to express love and caring. To hurt one's spouse is really injuring oneself—because the person's reliance on his or her spouse to help in time of difficulty has been stripped and reduced.

"I love you and I am in love with you."

Over many years of being in the gospel ministry, I have heard people use the phrase "I love you" many times, myself included. Many use it loosely to secure favors from others. The phrase has also fallen into the category of a mere salutation indicating courtesy. During my counseling sessions I spend some time discussing the difference between "I love you" and "I'm in love with you." "I love you" says, "See you later," but "I'm in love with you" says, "I want to go with you."

Love *Feel* and Love *Do*

At the beginning of a relationship the emotions of couples level off in many cases on the high side. This carries over into the early months of the marriage relationship. Then comes a phase of emotional tapering off. When this happens couples began wondering if the marriage is beginning to fall apart, if they are still loved or even wanted. The truth about feelings is that they come and go. Think in terms of an athletic team having what is commonly known as momentum, that is, everything seems to be going in the right direction.

Then something happens and a shift in momentum occurs. Now everything is going in favor of the other team until the pendulum of momentum swings back. The team generally stay together during a drop in momentum and work hard to swing the pendulum of momentum back in their favor. The point is clear: momentum, emotional energy or feelings, comes and goes.

This is just a part of the ebb and flow of life. Just because momentum shifts doesn't mean that you abandon the team. Why? The momentum inevitably comes back. The decision to remain on the team is not a momentum issue—it's a decision issue. That is why I say to couples that just because you don't have love *feel*, you must love *do* until love *feel* returns. Marriage is not based on a feeling—it is based on a decision. There may arise times when you will look at your spouse and have no feeling, nothing at that moment. Then something happens and you're back in the feeling zone again. But if you abandon the relationship abruptly for lack of feeling what you experienced at the beginning of the relationship, you need to reevaluate your decision-making process.

Marriage isn't automatic—it's work.

As my wife and I were watching airplanes land and take off, a pilot told us that there is a moment when the airplane reaches a point on the runway that is called "commitment"—at which the plane is traveling too fast to stop safely and *must* take off or else crash and burn.

If a marriage relationship is going to survive the test of time, there must be a high level of commitment from both spouses. Too often marriage is seen as a temporary arrangement. I have heard couples say, "If my spouse treats me in a way that's disrespectful, I'm done." Of course, I'm completely against spouses disrespecting each other in any way—but many walk away from their marriage relationship without due deliberation. That is, they fail to consider if there is an underlying issue causing the misbehavior. As I stated before, no person or marriage is perfect. I'm familiar with a pastor whose wife told him that she wanted a divorce. He responded by saying, "What are you going to tell the judge about your grounds for divorce?" He offered these suggestions: "I provide you with money, housing, protection, love, and concern." After some time of thinking this through, his wife said that he was right and changed her mind about filing for divorce.

Purpose to keep the passion (intense, driving, or overmastering feeling or conviction) of presence in your marriage. In short, let your spouse know that you are present.

I really like the quote by Sandra Bullock and her actor husband in the movie called the *The Blind Side*. A coach entered her home to discuss her pretend son attending the university that he represented. When the coach entered, one of Sandra's lines in the movie was that the coach was "good looking." Her husband in the movie said, "I'm standing right *here*." What a great line! Spouses must be extremely careful to avoid drifting to their sacred corners and erecting walls of self-justification for saying or doing things that might embarrass their spouses.

16

Distractions

Many things can be called attention-getters. The tragedy about distraction is that it can become non-recognizable by the person being distracted.

Based on definition, emotions, feelings, and a sense of satisfaction that has been exaggerated in this matter can be detrimental to a marriage relationship. I'm not saying that spouses cannot have a healthy interest apart from the marriage relationship. Nor am I saying that a spouse should restrict the other spouse from any and all healthy activities apart from the marriage relationship.

What I *am* saying is that spouses must be careful not to allow any activity to drive a wedge into the marriage relationship.

It is imperative that spouses give each other space to be creative and to recreate. No one wants to feel that he or she is trapped with no way of escape. Equally true is that no spouse wants to feel that he or she no longer matters. That's the concern that hoovers over distractions.

A spouse analyzes his or her value in the relationship to the distraction whether it is real or imagined. To ignore this dilemma is detrimental to the marriage relationship. Having an honest, fair, and open discussion of disruptive marital issues is always healthy. Whenever these issues are not addressed, one or both spouses suffer. Listen to the apostle Paul's discourse in the scripture below. Note his lecture on the potential for distraction and the demands within the marriage relationship.

> *Let the husband render unto the wife due benevolence: and likewise also the wife unto the husband. The wife hath not power of her own body, but the husband: and likewise also the husband hath not power of his own body, but the wife.* (1 Corinthians 7:3–4)

One of the dutiful responsibilities of a husband and wife is to freely and willingly engage in intercourse with each other. Yes, couples must respect each other in this matter, but arbitrarily denying each other is never healthy.

I have counseled individuals who have used this biblical act as leverage to secure a certain end or as punishment by way of refusal to engage in intercourse with their spouses. About thirty years ago a person called me and said that she was going to divorce her husband because he had committed adultery. After some time of discussion, it was revealed that she had refused to have intercourse with her husband. What the lady did not admit was her part in positioning her husband for sexual infidelity. It is without a doubt that he should not have committed adultery. It is also true that she should not have set her husband up for failure.

> *Defraud ye not one the other, except it be with consent for a time, that ye may give yourselves to fasting and prayer; and come together again, that Satan tempt you not for your incontinency.* (1 Corinthians 7:3–5)

Fraud involves depriving another person of someone of something by the use of deception." This is what the apostle Paul is driving at in a marriage relationship. Couples must be honest about their intentions while seeking the agreement or compliance from the other party, with the intent of resuming what was suspended.

> *But and if thou marry, thou hast not sinned; and if a virgin marry, she hath not sinned. Nevertheless such shall have trouble in the flesh: but I spare you.* (1 Corinthians 7:28)

> *But I would have you without carefulness. He that is unmarried careth for the things that belong to the Lord, how he may please the Lord: But he that is married careth for the things that are of the world, how he may please his wife. There is difference also between a wife and a*

> *virgin. The unmarried woman careth for the things of the Lord, that she may be holy both in body and in spirit: but she that is married careth for the things of the world, how she may please her husband. And this I speak for your own profit; not that I may cast a snare upon you, but for that which is comely, and that ye may attend upon the Lord without distraction.*
> (1 Corinthians 7:32–35)

Paul uses the word *care* several times in his discourse. He is making the case for clear communication and a willingness on the part of both spouses to accept the aspirations, tolerate, understand, yield to, and appreciate what their spouses would like to do in order to continue spiritual and physical development. In the marriage relationship space must be given to allow spouses to enjoy a healthy independence that will blossom into a healthy interdependency. When people walk in ownership of themselves, they can freely give of themselves.

Independence: the state of not looking to others for one's opinions or for guidance in conduct.

Interdependence: the state of being reciprocal or carried on between two people or things.

17

Jealousy

Jealousy is a word used to meaning the act of being intolerant or suspicious of any trace of rivalry or unfaithfulness between individuals. Words are like doors, which have two sides. Because of this two-sidedness or this dual track, jealousy can and must be viewed from both sides. One is suspicion— suspecting something wrong with or without proof. The other is validation—recognizing and establishing worth. Let's explore some the scriptures concerning jealousy.

> *For thou shalt worship no other god: for the Lord, whose name is Jealous, is a jealous God.*
> (Exodus 34:14)

The above verse is very clear in stating that God is a jealous God and that His name is jealous. Understanding that the word has two sides and observing the truth of the next set of scriptures, which clearly describe God's love for His creation, reveal the healthy side of jealousy.

For God so loved the world, that he gave his only begotten Son, that whosoever believeth in him should not perish, but have everlasting life.
(John 3:16)

But God commendeth his love toward us, in that, while we were yet sinners, Christ died for us. (Romans 5:8)

He that spared not his own Son, but delivered him up for us all, how shall he not with him also freely give us all things? (Romans 8:32)

Greater love hath no man than this, that a man lay down his life for his friends.
(John 15:13)

For I am jealous over you with godly jealousy: for I have espoused you to one husband, that I may present you as a chaste virgin to Christ.
(2 Corinthians 11:2)

A spouse who exhibits a positive or healthy jealousy is saying that there is no one living or dead who would love, protect, and provide the way he or she would. Therefore, this person does not want his or her spouse to be with anyone else by force, threat, or intimidation. The person wants to be in the marriage relationship because he or she has no doubt that the two are entering into a healthy love relationship.

God always has mankind's best interest at heart. He eternally knows that to have a healthy relationship with Him is eternally beneficial for all His creation as seen in the verses below.

> *For I know the thoughts that I think toward you, saith the Lord, thoughts of peace, and not of evil, to give you an expected end.*
> (Jeremiah 29:11)

> *See, I have set before thee this day life and good, and death and evil; In that I command thee this day to love the Lord thy God, to walk in his ways, and to keep his commandments and his statutes and his judgments, that thou mayest live and multiply: and the Lord thy God shall bless thee in the land whither thou goest to possess it.*
> (Deuteronomy 30:15–16)

> *I call heaven and earth to record this day against you, that I have set before you life and death, blessing and cursing: therefore choose life, that both thou and thy seed may live: That thou mayest love the Lord thy God, and that thou mayest obey his voice, and that thou mayest cleave unto him: for he is thy life, and the length of thy days: that thou mayest dwell in the land which the Lord sware unto thy fathers, to Abraham, to Isaac, and to Jacob, to give them.*
> (Deuteronomy 30:19–20)

In a counseling opportunity that was unsuccessful, a couple came into my office wanting to discuss principles to salvage their marriage. The husband had a belief system that did not allow him to receive any instructions from the Holy Scriptures. He began to instruct me to find alternative counseling sources.

I responded by saying, "Sir you came to me because your marriage is in jeopardy. I'm willing to help with you and your wife with the restoration process with the resources at my disposal." He refused. He and his wife with their broken relationship walked out of my office. While ultimately in charge of the kind of care he or she is willing to receive, the patient has to allow the doctor to apply his or her medical training to come to bear on the patient's illness.

God has given every person the internal ability to believe in Him and receive help in time of trouble or difficulties. It is our responsibility to actualize this gift. If we do not, we set in motion principles that will make life more difficult. Below are some scriptures for your consideration.

> *But without faith it is impossible to please him: for he that cometh to God must believe that he is, and that he is a rewarder of them that diligently seek him.* (Hebrews 11:6)

> *For I say, through the grace given unto me, to every man that is among you, not to think of himself more highly than he ought to think; but to think soberly, according as God hath dealt to every man the measure of faith.* (Romans 12:3)

> *The fool hath said in his heart, There is no God. Corrupt are they, and have done abominable iniquity: there is none that doeth good. God looked down from heaven upon the children of men, to see if there were any that did understand, that did seek God. Every one of them is gone back: they are altogether become filthy; there is none that doeth good, no, not one.*
> (Psalm 53:1–3)

Negative jealousy has been the ruin of many marriage relationships. A spouse can become so suspicious of the other spouse that day-to-day living is stressful. Jealousy can be real or imagined. I remember a person I was counseling who was absolutely convinced that infidelity had entered the person's marriage. I asked, "What definitive proof do you have that validates your spouse's infidelity?" The answer: "I don't have any definitive proof." Instead of doing the kind of things that would close the gaps in their marriage relationship, the suspicion continued. This marriage failed without any definitive evidence of infidelity. The marriage partner in this relationship said, "I can't take this anymore—I'm done." We should never do things that drive a person out of the marriage relationship. Healthy communication and trust, though fragile, must take priority. Silence is not always golden.

Negative jealousy for the most part assumes the worse. If a woman says, "I have a Hoover vacuum cleaner," negative jealousy says, "Who is he, and how long have this been going on?" I know of a situation whereby a husband would secretly follow his wife as she traveled from store to store. Her response was "I know he's following me. One day he'll finally be convinced that I have no desire to be unfaithful to him. Now we go shopping in separate cars."

> *For jealousy is the rage of a man: therefore he will not spare in the day of vengeance. He will not regard any ransom; neither will he rest content, though thou givest many gifts.*
> (Proverbs 6:34–35)

> *Set me as a seal upon thine heart, as a seal upon thine arm: for love is strong as death; jealousy is cruel as the grave: the coals thereof are coals of fire, which hath a most vehement flame.*
> (Song of Solomon 8:6)

> *As ye know how we exhorted and comforted and charged every one of you, as a father doth his children.* (1 Thessalonians 2:11)

> *Again the word of the Lord of hosts came to me, saying, Thus saith the Lord of hosts; I was jealous for Zion with great jealousy, and I was jealous for her with great fury. Thus saith the Lord; I am returned unto Zion, and will dwell in the midst of Jerusalem: and Jerusalem shall be called a city*

of truth; and the mountain of the Lord of hosts the holy mountain. (Zechariah 8:1–3)

Speak unto the children of Israel, and say unto them, If any man's wife go aside, and commit a trespass against him, And a man lie with her carnally, and it be hid from the eyes of her husband, and be kept close, and she be defiled, and there be no witness against her, neither she be taken with the manner; And the spirit of jealousy come upon him, and he be jealous of his wife, and she be defiled: or if the spirit of jealousy come upon him, and he be jealous of his wife, and she be not defiled. (Numbers 5:12–14)

Then the priest shall charge the woman with an oath of cursing, and the priest shall say unto the woman, The Lord make thee a curse and an oath among thy people, when the Lord doth make thy thigh to rot, and thy belly to swell; And this water that causeth the curse shall go into thy bowels, to make thy belly to swell, and thy thigh to rot: And the woman shall say, Amen, amen. And the priest shall write these curses in a book, and he shall blot them out with the bitter water: And he shall cause the woman to drink the bitter water that causeth the curse: and the water that causeth the curse shall enter into her, and become bitter. Then the priest shall take the jealousy offering out of the woman's hand, and shall wave the offering before the Lord, and offer it upon the altar: And the priest shall take an handful of the offering, even the memorial thereof, and burn it upon the altar, and afterward shall cause the woman to drink the water. And when he hath made her to drink the water, then it shall come to pass, that, if she be defiled, and have done trespass against her husband, that the water that causeth the curse shall enter into her, and become bitter, and her belly shall swell, and her thigh shall rot: and the woman shall be a curse among her people. And if the woman be not defiled, but be clean; then she shall be free, and shall conceive seed. This is the law of jealousies, when a wife goeth aside to another instead of her husband, and is defiled. (Numbers 5:21–29)

I think we can agree that the previous scenario can be reversed—the wife can have suspicions about her husband. I'm familiar with a situation in which a husband had several affairs. His wife in her anger decided to get even with him by having an affair of her own and told him why she did it. The husband was so angry that he could not forgive her even though she was willing to forgive him.

Society has become biased in that it is acceptable for a man to attend a strip club while his wife is at home with the children. If anything, the man should be setting the example of fidelity and trustworthiness for his wife, his children, and his community.

18

Integrity

Integrity refers *to* the quality of honesty and upholding high moral principles. I would say that it is inevitable that a spouse will eventually meet someone who has the qualities or traits that are very much like those of his or her spouse. Equally so, a spouse will inevitably meet or see someone who is attractive physically. These encounters are not predictive but coincidental. Regardless of where you are in your marriage relationship—good, bad, ugly, or critical—you're still married. There must be a determination to avoid any wanted or unwanted relationship development. The focus must be to do whatever possible to maintain or restore a marriage relationship to health. Below are several scriptures that emphasize faithfulness to one's spouse.

> *For the lips of an immoral woman are as sweet as honey,*
> *and her mouth is smoother than oil.*
> *But in the end she is as bitter as poison,*
> *as dangerous as a double-edged sword.*

Her feet go down to death;
   her steps lead straight to the grave.
For she cares nothing about the path to life.
   She staggers down a crooked trail and doesn't realize it.
So now, my sons, listen to me.
   Never stray from what I am about to say:
Stay away from her!
   Don't go near the door of her house!
If you do, you will lose your honor
   and will lose to merciless people all you have achieved.
Strangers will consume your wealth,
   and someone else will enjoy the fruit of your labor.
In the end you will groan in anguish
   when disease consumes your body.
(Proverbs 5:3–11 NLT)

You will say, "How I hated discipline!
   If only I had not ignored all the warnings!
Oh, why didn't I listen to my teachers?
   Why didn't I pay attention to my instructors?
I have come to the brink of utter ruin,
   and now I must face public disgrace."
Drink water from your own well—
   share your love only with your wife.
Why spill the water of your springs in the streets,
   having sex with just anyone?
You should reserve it for yourselves.
   Never share it with strangers.
Let your wife be a fountain of blessing for you.
   Rejoice in the wife of your youth.

> *She is a loving deer, a graceful doe.*
>   *Let her breasts satisfy you always.*
>   *May you always be captivated by her love.*
> *Why be captivated, my son, by an immoral woman,*
> *or fondle the breasts of a promiscuous woman?*
> (Proverbs 5:12–20 NLT)

> *The man who finds a wife finds a treasure, and he receives favor from the Lord.*
> (Proverbs 18:22 NLT)

> *Live joyfully with the wife whom thou lovest all the days of the life of thy vanity, which he hath given thee under the sun, all the days of thy vanity: for that is thy portion in this life, and in thy labour which thou takest under the sun.*
> (Ecclesiastes 9:9)

As noted earlier, some people rationalize their sexual misbehavior by claiming that they're only acting out the desires that God put within them. However, it is equally true that God allowed mankind use of fire. With the use of fire comes responsibility. The use of fire has certain parameters, such as where, when, how, and why it is used. Typically, when we hear of structural fires, forest fires, and industrial fires, they often happened because something controllable was ignored or violated.

Just because human beings are not perfect does not give them license to purposely act irresponsible. Fire must be used in a responsible manner—so it is with mankind's sexual desire. Fire can both warm a house and burn it down.

> *Can a man take fire in his bosom, and his clothes not be burned? Can one go upon hot coals, and his feet not be burned? So he that goeth in to his neighbour's wife; whosoever toucheth her shall not be innocent.* (Proverbs 6:27–29)

> *Not as though I had already attained, either were already perfect: but I follow after, if that I may apprehend that for which also I am apprehended of Christ Jesus.* (Philippians 3:12)

> *A double minded man is unstable in all his ways.* (James 1:8)

> *And Ruth said, Intreat me not to leave thee, or to return from following after thee: for whither thou goest, I will go; and where thou lodgest, I will lodge: thy people shall be my people, and thy God my God: Where thou diest, will I die, and there will I be buried: the Lord do so to me, and more also, if ought but death part thee and me.* (Ruth 1:16–17)

Many people are journeying toward marriage without really understanding marriage *commitment,* which will affect the rest of their lives. Without this understanding, undue difficulties will be a constant throughout the marriage relationship. If a husband wants his wife to treat him like a king, he must treat her like a queen.

The common expression "It's thought that counts" must be redefined in this respect. If expressing love were just a thought, then the actual expressions of love in a practical and tangible way could be eliminated.

> *For God so loved the world, that he gave his only begotten Son, that whosoever believeth in him should not perish, but have everlasting life.* (John 3:16)

God's love is evidenced by His actions. That action includes the giving of His Son to die for the sins of mankind, thereby providing opportunity for anyone and everyone to experience eternal life.

> *For God sent not his Son into the world to condemn the world; but that the world through him might be saved.* (John 3:17)

Condemn means "to declare unfit; to declare damaged and irreparable." It is not our job to look for faults in our spouses. If you can find something wrong with a person, it stands to reason that you can find something right or good as well.

A selfish attitude in a relationship will ultimately destroy it. This is the "consumer mentality. Consider the scripture listed below in light of the marriage concept:

> *And he spake a parable unto them, saying, The ground of a certain rich man brought forth plentifully: And he thought within himself, saying, What shall I do, because I have no room where to bestow my fruits? And he said, This will I do: I will pull down my barns, and build greater; and there will I bestow all my fruits and my goods. And I will say to my soul, Soul, thou hast much goods laid up for many years; take thine ease, eat, drink, and be merry. But God said unto him, Thou fool, this night thy soul shall be required of thee: then whose shall those things be, which thou hast provided?* (Luke 12:16–20)

In order to maintain strong marriages, couples must gain greater insights concerning Christ. In addition to providing redemption, Jesus came into the world to present opportunities for salvation (deliverance) financially, spiritually, socially, relationally, morally, ethically, temperamentally, psychologically, sexually, and so on.

> *If thou shalt confess with thy mouth the Lord Jesus, and shalt believe in thine heart that God hath raised him from the dead, thou shalt be*

saved. For with the heart man believeth unto righteousness; and with the mouth confession is made unto salvation. For the scripture saith, Whosoever believeth on him shall not be ashamed. (Romans 10:9–11)

It's not enough simply to *know* the right thing to do. One must *do* what he or she knows is the right thing to do.

> **In marriage you look out not only for your own personal interests but also for those of the other person.**

19

A Digest of Marriage Concepts

I have called the first five years of marriage "the discovery stage." This is a time frame when couples discover traits, behaviors, and characteristics of each other that were overlooked or missed during their relationship development. This can also be called the "if only I had known" phase.

I call the second five years "the recovery stage." In this stage couples get their second wind, take a deep breath, and gather themselves under the umbrella of marriage and are determined to stay married. This can also be called the "self-sacrifice" phase.

The third five years I call "the redefining stage." This is when couples make the necessary adjustments for the continuance of the marriage relationship. The downside of this stage is that the adjustment may or may not be healthy. This can also be called the "whatever it takes" phase.

The fourth five years I refer to as "the ready stage." This a time when couples have a good understanding of each other and themselves in the context of marriage. Now they can become more productive, not competitive but complementary to each other whether they're in the same location or temporarily away from each other.

Selection of a spouse must be based primarily on spiritual qualities such as intellect, personality, belief system, morals, character, emotional stability, ethics, and so on. There's no doubt that our physical attributes will change as we get older.

> *But the Lord said unto Samuel, Look not on his countenance, or on the height of his stature; because I have refused him: for the Lord seeth not as man seeth; for man looketh on the outward appearance, but the Lord looketh on the heart.* (1 Samuel 16:7)

When a person selects a potential spouse primarily from physical attractiveness without any consideration of the person's character, there may be some future disappointment. It's amazing what individuals value in the physical attributes that stimulate a person's interest in another person. The scriptures below contain principles to be considered during the marriage journey.

> *He said to them, "You are the ones who justify yourselves in the eyes of others, but God knows your hearts. What people highly value is detestable in God's sight.* (Luke 16:15 NLT)

But let it be the hidden man of the heart, in that which is not corruptible, even the ornament of a meek and quiet spirit, which is in the sight of God of great price. (1 Peter 3:4)

This is the thing which the Lord doth command concerning the daughters of Zelophehad, saying, Let them marry to whom they think best; only to the family of the tribe of their father shall they marry. (Numbers 36:6)

Whether therefore ye eat, or drink, or whatsoever ye do, do all to the glory of God. (1 Corinthians 10:31)

According to Norman Cousins, "A man or woman cannot be comfortable without his or her own approval." Romance is an emotional attraction to a person. Marriage reveals who we really are (honest, dishonest, sincere, not sincere, humble, prideful). What individuals take into the relationship determines what issues must be dealt with. Whatever you take onto the field is what you must play with. However a person practices is how the person plays.

We then that are strong ought to bear the infirmities of the weak, and not to please ourselves. Let every one of us please his neighbour for his good to edification. For even Christ pleased not

himself; but, as it is written, The reproaches of them that reproached thee fell on me.
(Romans 15:1–3)

Biblical reality is the ability to release the inner qualities that represent the heart of God. Marriage is work, not automation. Married couples must report to work every day. To have a good night you must have a good morning. Marriage is never what we think or imagine. Spouses should constantly search for ways to reveal their love and unpackage their self-worth.

Marriage is a lifelong agreement between a male and female before God and affirmed by a minister of the gospel, before witnesses, that they will remain life partners until death, abstaining from any relationships that will hinder or jeopardize their sacred union. The purpose of the witnesses and those in attendance is to remind the bride and groom in the days ahead of their marital commitment.

Marriage is a covenant that includes God, making it a solemn agreement to do or keep from doing specific things. The origin and binding principles of the covenant are contained in God's Word. While discussing this principle with one couple, I asked them this question: "Have you invited God to your wedding?" The lady said, "I'll be mailing out the invitation." I simply stared and repeated my question. Both said no. It is a strange thing for God to be left out of the invitation stage, having instituted or created marriage in the first place.

A. What marriage is

1. A *gift*. Your spouse is the finest gift you have ever received. A gift is an item selected with care and consideration. Its purpose is to delight and fulfill the receiver, an expression of deep feelings on the part of the giver.

   Gifts that are often appreciated the most are not the most expensive but those reflecting the investment of the giver in considering the desires of the other person, including the presentation of the sacrifice to provide the gift.

   A gift is given as an expression of our love. It is not based on whether the recipient deserves it or not—our giving is an act of grace.

2. Opportunity for love to be *learned*.

   a. Love will not be silent.

   b. Love sees only the beautiful.

   c. Love involves giving and receiving.

   d. Love is enhanced by friendship.

   e. Love risks the possibility of pain.

   f. Love is very difficult to express in words.

   g. Love must be given freely.

   h. True love is priceless.

   i. Love is the key that opens closed doors.

3. Marriage is a *journey*, which includes many choices. We are responsible for those choices.
4. Marriage is more often *influenced by unresolved issues from our past* than we realize.
5. Marriage is a call to *friendship*.
6. Marriage is a call to *suffering*. I was told by one of my single students that there are three rings in the marriage relationship, namely the engagement ring, wedding ring, and the suffe*ring*. Marriage definitely includes some unpleasant moments.
7. Marriage is a *refining* process. It is an opportunity to be refined by God into the person He wants you to be.
8. Marriage is not an event but a *way of life*.
9. Marriage involves *intimacy* in all areas for it to be fulfilling.
10. Marriage is a call to *servanthood*.
11. Take *walks of intimacy*.
12. God will *never leave you alone*. Marriage declares the same truth.
13. Once you decide to love there is *no turning back*.

> **The wedding ends but marriage goes on.**

> **Getting to know the person you're going to marry is extremely important. Why? You're marrying a *stranger*.**

- God performed the first wedding.
- God made woman by taking a rib from man and closed up the flesh. This process required the man to be put to sleep.
- In marriage God reopens man and begins the process of putting the woman back into the man.
- Marriage includes being in a place where love is constant.
- Marriage is a pressure that can be handled only by love.
- Being married is not to be taken off the front lines of love but rather to be plunged into it.
- A continuous daily renewal is needed to remain married.
- Marriage is an impossible adventure that be accomplished only through the grace of God. "For with God nothing shall be impossible" (Luke 1:37).
- To go forward from love to marriage is to take a step of faith. It is to stake life upon a spiritual experience trust.

- We cannot take time off from breathing. In like manner we cannot take time off from being married.

- Love attacks and destroys pride. Love creates the only safe ground upon which self-assertion may begin to be surrendered.

- The energy of love flows from being loved in return. Kinetic energy movement causes energy, and energy causes movement.

> **Pride is an unduly high opinion of oneself, an exaggerated self-esteem. By contrast, a proper respect for oneself and others, a sense of one's own self-worth, is healthy.**

B. Personal attitudes as they relate to marriage

- Most of your emotions, such as depression, guilt, and worry, are initiated and escalated by self-talk.

- The way you behave toward your spouse is determined by your self-talk.

- What you say and how you say it is a direct expression of your self-talk.

- A positive attitude toward life will generate positive self-talk.
- A negative attitude toward life will generate negative self-talk.
- The chief characteristic of negative thought is that it is generally wrong.
- Negatives are developed in the dark.
- Negative self-talk does not reflect reality but rather insecurity, inadequacy, and fears.
- If you give in to negative thoughts without countering them and evaluating them, the results will be negative.
- Self-talk creates mental pictures in our minds and then the imagination is called into action.
- Good intimacy does not make for a good marriage. But a good marriage makes for good intimacy.
- Help each other with anniversary and birthday dates

Be not deceived; God is not mocked: for whatsoever a man soweth, that shall he also reap. (Galatians 6:7)

Charity never faileth: but whether there be prophecies, they shall fail; whether there be tongues, they shall cease; whether there be knowledge, it shall vanish away. And now abideth faith, hope, charity, these three; but the greatest of these is charity. (1 Corinthians 13:8, 13)

C. The importance of biblical principles for the survival of a marriage

- **Whenever you transgress God's principles, the marriage relationship will be jeopardized.**

> **Don't come off your honeymoon!**

Wives, submit yourselves unto your own husbands, as unto the Lord. For the husband is the head of the wife, even as Christ is the head of the church: and he is the saviour of the body. Therefore as the church is subject unto Christ, so let the wives be to their own husbands in every thing. Husbands, love your wives, even as Christ also loved the church, and gave himself for it; That he might sanctify and cleanse it with the washing of water by the word, That he might present it to himself a glorious church, not having spot, or wrinkle, or any such thing; but that it should be holy and without blemish. So ought men to love their wives as their own bodies. He that loveth his wife loveth himself. For no man ever yet hated his own flesh; but nourisheth and cherisheth it, even as the Lord the church: For we are members of his body, of his flesh, and of his bones. For this cause shall a man leave his father and mother, and shall be joined unto his wife, and they two shall be one flesh. This is a great mystery: but I speak concerning Christ and the church. Nevertheless let every one of you in particular so love his wife even as himself; and the wife see that she reverence her husband. (Ephesians 5:22–33, emphasis added)

And when the woman saw that the tree was good for food, and that it was pleasant to the eyes, and a tree to be desired to make one wise, she took of the fruit thereof, and did eat, and gave also unto her husband with her; and he did eat. (Genesis 3:6)

The woman listened to the serpent and Adam listened to his wife, but no one listened to God.

D. The importance of the husband listening to his wife

And David said to Abigail, Blessed be the Lord God of Israel, which sent thee this day to meet me: And blessed be thy advice, and

blessed be thou, which hast kept me this day from coming to shed blood, and from avenging myself with mine own hand. For in very deed, as the Lord God of Israel liveth, which hath kept me back from hurting thee, except thou hadst hasted and come to meet me, surely there had not been left unto Nabal by the morning light any that pisseth against the wall.
(1 Samuel 25:32–34)

And Sarah saw the son of Hagar the Egyptian, which she had born unto Abraham, mocking. Wherefore she said unto Abraham, Cast out this bondwoman and her son: for the son of this bondwoman shall not be heir with my son, even with Isaac. And the thing was very grievous in Abraham's sight because of his son. And God said unto Abraham, Let it not be grievous in thy sight because of the lad, and because of thy bondwoman; in all that Sarah hath said unto thee, hearken unto her voice; for in Isaac shall thy seed be called. (Genesis 21:9–12)

And Manoah said unto his wife, We shall surely die, because we have seen God. But his wife said unto him, If the Lord were pleased to kill us, he would not have received a burnt offering and a meat offering at our hands, neither would he have shewed us all these things, nor would as at this time have told us such things as these. (Judges 13:22–23)

The woman blamed the serpent and the man blamed the woman—and secretly they both blamed God.

> **People in many cases want to have the upper hand or control.**

Nevertheless, to avoid fornication, let every man have his own wife, and let every woman have her own husband. (1 Corinthians 7:2)

Marriage is honorable in all, and the bed undefiled: but whoremongers and adulterers God will judge. (Hebrews 13:4)

- It can be a great shock for a couple to discover how quickly romantic love is exhausted and how little they really know or understand about each other.
- We must learn to love with our mouths and voices as well as with our eyes, flesh, hearts, and brains.

- Marriage is the closest bond that is possible between two human beings.

- People love weddings because it is one of the very few occasions when the formation of a true, lasting, and real bond between two human beings may be witnessed.

- A good marriage is the closest thing on earth to the realization of a practical, enduring, and loving coexistence between people.

- A good marriage is the foundation of society.

- History has revealed that not just any love can justify and bless a marriage.

- The love of God is the only love that can sustain a marriage.

- If a person is not willing to abandon himself or herself and to completely love, especially exhibiting the love of God, then forget it.

- Silence and rejection are a punishment that causes a spouse to bleed. Stop the bleeding before it's too late.

> **Marriage is designed to point sinners to God.**

This is the thing which the Lord doth command concerning the daughters of Zelophehad, saying, Let them marry to whom they think best; only to the family of the tribe of their father shall they marry. (Numbers 36:6)

Marriage is ordained to be between a male and female, not an animal or inanimate object.

Marriage seems to specialize at times in radically de-emphasizing the similarities between marriage partners while wildly exaggerating the differences.

Some people are amazed that they are together at all. They realize that something greater than themselves is holding the marriage together.

Now the Spirit speaketh expressly, that in the latter times some shall depart from the faith, giving heed to seducing spirits, and doctrines of devils; Speaking lies in hypocrisy; having their conscience seared with a hot iron; Forbidding to marry, and commanding to abstain from meats, which God hath created to be received with thanksgiving of them which believe and know the truth. (1 Timothy 4:1–3)

Marriage is God's way of expressing His love through human beings.

> **The purpose of procreation is not just to have children but to fill the earth with godly values.**

Lo, children are an heritage of the Lord: and the fruit of the womb is his reward.
(Psalm 127:3)

- Marriage is living with glory, with a mystery that is fully visible, with a flesh-and-blood person who can be touched and held.
- To be married is to be confronted intimately day after day with the mystery of life outside of one's self. You are not alone.
- There is nevertheless something in marriage that defies being taken for granted.
- It is a source of enormous human frustration because the spouse cannot fulfill all the needs of the other spouse.
- No one can love us as God does and no one can be the sort of friend to us that God is.

- The extra longing of the human heart is fulfilled only by God. Some people seek to fulfill this area on the human level.
- Marriage is really choosing the closeness of God in the form of a close relationship with another person.
- The marriage relationship is the axis around which all family relationships are found.

"Love is an act of endless forgiveness, a tender look which becomes a habit" (Peter Ustinov).

"A happy marriage is the union of two good forgivers" (Robert Quillen).

"Love doesn't make the world go round. Love is what makes the ride worthwhile" (Franklin P. Jones).

"Love is the greatest gift when given. It is the highest honor when received" (Fawn Weaver).

"Success in marriage does not come merely through finding the right mate but through being the right mate" (Barnett R. Brickner).

> **"By the family broken, by the family healed"** points out the power of a family to hurt or to heal its members.

Whether therefore ye eat, or drink, or whatsoever ye do, do all to the glory of God. Give none offence, neither to the Jews, nor to the Gentiles, nor to the church of God: Even as I please all men in all things, not seeking mine own profit, but the profit of many, that they may be saved.
(1 Corinthians 10:31–33)

- The husband is to position himself between his wife and whatever is causing her frustration.
- The husband is to lovingly lead his wife to Christ by way of example.
- A truly loving husband will regard his wife as a completely equal partner in everything that concerns their lives.
- Loving leadership affirms, defers, shares, encourages, and stimulates.
- Loving leadership delights to delegate without demanding.

Then Joseph her husband, being a just man, and not willing to make her a public example, was minded to put her away privily.
(Matthew 1:19)

- **Marriage is shared *pain*.**

Likewise, ye husbands, dwell with them according to knowledge, giving honour unto the wife, as unto the weaker vessel, and as being heirs together of the grace of life; that your prayers be not hindered. (1 Peter 3:7)

"Don't compare your love story to those you watch in movie theaters or television. They're written by screenwriters—yours is written by God" (unknown).

"To the world you may be one person, but to one person you may be the world" (unknown).

"The most desired gift of love is not diamonds or roses or chocolate. It's focused attention" (Rick Warren).

"A happy man married the girl he loves; a happier man loves the girl he marries" (Susan Douglas).

"Love put the fun in together, the sad in apart, and the joy in a heart" (anonymous).

"*Love says, 'The only place I want to be with you is closer'*" (unknown).

"*The greatest gift a father can give his children is to love their mother*" (John Wooden).

Blessed is every one that feareth the Lord; that walketh in his ways. For thou shalt eat the labour of thine hands: happy shalt thou be, and it shall be well with thee. Thy wife shall be as a fruitful vine by the sides of thine house: thy children like olive plants round about thy table. Behold, that thus shall the man be blessed that feareth the Lord. (Psalm 128:1–4)

Live joyfully with the wife whom thou lovest all the days of the life of thy vanity, which he hath given thee under the sun, all the days of thy vanity: for that is thy portion in this life, and in thy labour which thou takest under the sun. (Ecclesiastes 9:9)

20

Dialogue

Let your speech be always with grace, seasoned with salt, that ye may know how ye ought to answer every man. (Colossians 4:6)

A soft answer turneth away wrath: but grievous words stir up anger. (Proverbs 15:1)

- **Dialogue must be mutual, and the parties must be relentless.**
- **There is risk when entering conversation.**
- **Communication means life or death to individuals.**
- **Individuals must take responsibility for their roles in the conversation.**
- **To speak the word of love is to be loved as well as to love.**
- **The relationship between married couples reveals the indispensable need for dialogue.**

- To give someone a tongue-lashing is not healthy communication.

- Dialogue in marriage expresses mutual respect and defuses frustrations.

- Dialogue must speak out of conviction into the conviction of another with a sense of possibilities between them.

- Dialogue produces discovery and opens the door to the mystery of individuals.

- The most important thing about dialogue between Christians is that God is present to purify and transform both.

- A barrier to communication is something that keeps meanings from meeting.

- Communication is often hindered because people think it is easy.

- Communication occurs when both parties offer affirmation.

- A word means what the speaker intends it to mean, but the person hearing it may hear something different.

- Some people struggle with communication because they become defensive.

- The purpose of communication is not to seduce or exploit.

- **Communication helps individuals make responsible decisions.**
- **A decision to say no is as much a part of dialogue as a decision to say yes.**
- **The Word of God must be included in the dialogue process.**
- **Seek to understand before you seek to be understood.**

Dialogue's underlying principle:
Give without pretense

This means that we enter into relationship not for the purpose of gaining but for giving, with the prayer that we may lose our pretensions, our defensive need to justify ourselves, and gain instead a reassurance of life by having it affirmed in our relationship with another.

21

Divorce

Divorce is the result of what could have been. The pain of experiencing a divorce is like throwing a rock into a body of water. When it hits the water from the point of impact, energy circles began radiating outward. So it is when divorce takes place. Not only is the couple affected, but the effect of the divorce spreads outward. If the couple has children, these dear ones will also experience the drags of divorce.

It is so sad when a marriage has entered a downward spiral so severe that the only remedy is for the couple to separate or divorce. This a not only a critical and emotional crisis but also a sensitive arena in which the wrong advice could mean life or death for someone. The bottled-up pain that led to the separation or divorce lies under a thin layer of self-control.

Thirty-five years ago a lady separated from her husband because she was experiencing extreme marital stress. She asked a minister for advice. He told her that he could not tell her what to do concerning returning to her home and husband. She sought the advice of another minister, who told that it was her civil and Christian duty to return to her husband immediately. She did so. Sadly, that night she shot her husband to death, emptying a revolver into her husband's body. The emotional pain that she was experiencing searched for an outlet or opportunity and found one. The scripture below gives us some rationale as to why divorce happens.

> *When a man hath taken a wife, and married her, and it come to pass that she find no favour in his eyes, because he hath found some uncleanness in her: then let him write her a bill of divorcement, and give it in her hand, and send her out of his house. And when she is departed out of his house, she may go and be another man's wife. And if the latter husband hate her, and write her a bill of divorcement, and giveth it in her hand, and sendeth her out of his house; or if the latter husband die, which took her to be his wife; Her former husband, which sent her away, may not take her again to be his wife, after that she is defiled; for that is abomination before the Lord: and thou shalt not cause the land to sin, which the Lord thy God giveth thee for an inheritance.*
> (Deuteronomy 24:1–4)

The above verses emphasize the selfish attitudes of a man in regard to his wife. The scripture does not reveal the pain and embarrassment the woman may have experienced, and the situation can be reversed as well—it's true that a woman can be just as selfish and men can be embarrassed and experience pain as a marriage relationship deteriorates.

> *"I hate divorce!" says the Lord, the God of Israel. "To divorce your wife is to overwhelm her with cruelty," says the Lord of Heaven's Armies. "So guard your heart; do not be unfaithful to your wife." You have wearied the Lord with your words. "How have we wearied him?" you ask. You have wearied him by saying that all who do evil are good in the Lord's sight, and he is pleased with them. You have wearied him by asking, "Where is the God of justice?"*
> (Malachi 2:16–17 NLT)

Even though God hates divorce, it is a fact, that divorce happens, which He recognizes. Again, this is not the ideal but rather the antithesis. Ideally, marriage is one man and one woman for life or until death separates them.

> *Then Joseph her husband, being a just man, and not willing to make her a public example, was minded to put her away privily. But while he thought on these things, behold, the angel of*

> *the Lord appeared unto him in a dream, saying, Joseph, thou son of David, fear not to take unto thee Mary thy wife: for that which is conceived in her is of the Holy Ghost.* (Matthew 1:19–20)

Joseph sought the best interest for Mary. He was very reasonable in his actions toward her. As well, he was open to what God was saying to him through an angel, which means "messenger." In order for a marriage to be successful, this concept of listening to God and following His principles is paramount.

> *Some Pharisees came to him to test him. They asked, "Is it lawful for a man to divorce his wife for any and every reason?"*
> (Matthew 19:3 NIV)

> *Jesus replied, "Moses permitted you to divorce your wives because your hearts were hard. But it was not this way from the beginning. I tell you that anyone who divorces his wife, except for sexual immorality, and marries another woman commits adultery." The disciples said to him, "If this is the situation between a husband and wife, it is better not to marry." Jesus replied, "Not everyone can accept this word, but only those to whom it has been given."*
> (Matthew 19:8–11 NIV)

To the married I give this command (not I, but the Lord): A wife must not separate from her husband. But if she does, she must remain unmarried or else be reconciled to her husband. And a husband must not divorce his wife. To the rest I say this (I, not the Lord): If any brother has a wife who is not a believer and she is willing to live with him, he must not divorce her. And if a woman has a husband who is not a believer and he is willing to live with her, she must not divorce him. For the unbelieving husband has been sanctified through his wife, and the unbelieving wife has been sanctified through her believing husband. Otherwise your children would be unclean, but as it is, they are holy. But if the unbeliever leaves, let it be so. The brother or the sister is not bound in such circumstances; God has called us to live in peace. How do you know, wife, whether you will save your husband? Or, how do you know, husband, whether you will save your wife? Nevertheless, each person should live as a believer in whatever situation the Lord has assigned to them, just as God has called them. This is the rule I lay down in all the churches.

(1 Corinthians 7:10–17 NIV)

Below are some dynamics that are associated with divorce:

1. **Denial**
2. **Anger**
3. **Bargaining**
4. **Depression**
5. **Acceptance**

(These preceding five items are from Elisabeth Kübler-Ross: *On Death and Dying*)

6. **Discouragement**
7. **Trust issues**
8. **Uncertainty about marital success**
9. **Feeling deceived**
10. **Deep-seated anger**
11. **Traumatized children**
12. **Embarrassment**
13. **Blaming God**
14. **Pointing the finger**
15. **Refusing to accept culpability**
16. **Child custody**
17. **Financial adjustments**
18. **Dividing of assets**
19. **Offering explanations to friends and family**
20. **Avoidance**

Within the many principles of God is the principle of forgiveness and pardon. It is possible for a divorced person not to remain shattered and alone. God forgives and pardons. His challenge to mankind is that they learn from past mistakes and determine to follow His principles for marital successful moving forward. The following scriptures bear out these concepts:

> *Let the wicked forsake his way, and the unrighteous man his thoughts: and let him return unto the Lord, and he will have mercy upon him; and to our God, for he will abundantly pardon. For my thoughts are not your thoughts, neither are your ways my ways, saith the Lord. For as the heavens are higher than the earth, so are my ways higher than your ways, and my thoughts than your thoughts.* (Isaiah 55:7–9)

> *And he that was healed wist not who it was: for Jesus had conveyed himself away, a multitude being in that place. Afterward Jesus findeth him in the temple, and said unto him, Behold, thou art made whole: sin no more, lest a worse thing come unto thee.* (John 5:13–14)

> *If we confess our sins, he is faithful and just to forgive us our sins, and to cleanse us from all unrighteousness. If we say that we have not sinned, we make him a liar, and his word is not in us.* (1 John 1:9–10)

Therefore to him that knoweth to do good, and doeth it not, to him it is sin. (James 4:17)

Whosoever committeth sin transgresseth also the law: for sin is the transgression of the law.
(1 John 3:4)

The thief cometh not, but for to steal, and to kill, and to destroy: I am come that they might have life, and that they might have it more abundantly. (John 10:10)

And Jesus returned in the power of the Spirit into Galilee: and there went out a fame of him through all the region round about. And he taught in their synagogues, being glorified of all. And he came to Nazareth, where he had been brought up: and, as his custom was, he went into the synagogue on the sabbath day, and stood up for to read. And there was delivered unto him the book of the prophet Esaias. And when he had opened the book, he found the place where it was written, The Spirit of the Lord is upon me, because he hath anointed me to preach the gospel to the poor; he hath sent me to heal the brokenhearted, to preach deliverance to the captives, and recovering of sight to the blind, to set at liberty them that are bruised.
(Luke 4:14–18)

For God sent not his Son into the world to condemn the world; but that the world through him might be saved. (John 3:17)

Synopsis about marriage

- **Marriage is God's idea.**

    And the Lord God said, It is not good that the man should be alone; I will make him an help meet for him. And out of the ground the Lord God formed every beast of the field, and every fowl of the air; and brought them unto Adam to see what he would call them: and whatsoever Adam called every living creature, that was the name thereof. And Adam gave names to all cattle, and to the fowl of the air, and to every beast of the field; but for Adam there was not found an help meet for him. And the Lord God caused a deep sleep to fall upon Adam, and he slept: and he took one of his ribs, and closed up the flesh instead thereof; And the rib, which the Lord God had taken from man, made he a woman, and brought her unto the man. And Adam said, This is now bone of my bones, and flesh of my flesh: she shall be called Woman, because she was taken out of Man. Therefore shall a man leave his father and his mother, and shall cleave unto his wife: and they shall be one flesh.

    (Genesis 2:18–24)

- **Commitment is essential for a successful marriage.**

  And they called Rebekah, and said unto her, Wilt thou go with this man? And she said, I will go. And they sent away Rebekah their sister, and her nurse, and Abraham's servant, and his men. And they blessed Rebekah, and said unto her, Thou art our sister, be thou the mother of thousands of millions, and let thy seed possess the gate of those which hate them. (Genesis 24:58–60)

- **Romance is important in the marriage relationship.**

  Thou hast ravished my heart, my sister, my spouse; thou hast ravished my heart with one of thine eyes, with one chain of thy neck. How fair is thy love, my sister, my spouse! how much better is thy love than wine! and the smell of thine ointments than all spices!
  (Song of Solomon 4:9–10)

- **Marriage has times of great joy.**

  Thus saith the Lord; Again there shall be heard in this place, which ye say shall be desolate without man and without beast, even in the cities of Judah, and in the streets of Jerusalem, that are desolate, without man, and without inhabitant, and without beast, The voice of joy, and the voice of gladness, the voice of the bridegroom, and the

> voice of the bride, the voice of them that shall say, Praise the Lord of hosts: for the Lord is good; for his mercy endureth for ever: and of them that shall bring the sacrifice of praise into the house of the Lord. For I will cause to return the captivity of the land, as at the first, saith the Lord.
> (Jeremiah 33:10–11)

- **Marriage creates the best environment in which to raise children.**

  > Yet ye say, Wherefore? Because the Lord hath been witness between thee and the wife of thy youth, against whom thou hast dealt treacherously: yet is she thy companion, and the wife of thy covenant. And did not he make one? Yet had he the residue of the spirit. And wherefore one? That he might seek a godly seed. Therefore take heed to your spirit, and let none deal treacherously against the wife of his youth.
  > (Malachi 2:14–15)

- **Unfaithfulness breaks the bond of trust, which is the foundation of relationships.**

  > But I say unto you, That whosoever shall put away his wife, saving for the cause of fornication, causeth her to commit adultery: and whosoever shall marry her that is divorced committeth adultery. (Matthew 5:32)

- **Forgiveness starts a new cycle for human relationships.**

  Let the wicked forsake his way, and the unrighteous man his thoughts: and let him return unto the Lord, and he will have mercy upon him; and to our God, for he will abundantly pardon. For my thoughts are not your thoughts, neither are your ways my ways, saith the Lord. (Isaiah 55:7–8)

- **Marriage is designed for a lifelong commitment or until the death of a spouse.**

  Wherefore they are no more twain, but one flesh. What therefore God hath joined together, let not man put asunder. (Matthew 19:6)

  For the woman which hath an husband is bound by the law to her husband so long as he liveth; but if the husband be dead, she is loosed from the law of her husband. So then if, while her husband liveth, she be married to another man, she shall be called an adulteress: but if her husband be dead, she is free from that law; so that she is no adulteress, though she be married to another man. (Isaiah 7:2–3)

- **Marriage is based on the love principle, not feeling-based, and is a symbol of Christ and the church.**

  Submitting yourselves one to another in the fear of God. Wives, submit yourselves unto your own husbands, as unto the Lord. For the husband is the head of the wife, even as Christ is the head of the church: and he is the saviour of the body. Therefore as the church is subject unto Christ, so let the wives be to their own husbands in every thing. Husbands, love your wives, even as Christ also loved the church, and gave himself for it; That he might sanctify and cleanse it with the washing of water by the word, That he might present it to himself a glorious church, not having spot, or wrinkle, or any such thing; but that it should be holy and without blemish. So ought men to love their wives as their own bodies. He that loveth his wife loveth himself. For no man ever yet hated his own flesh; but nourisheth and cherisheth it, even as the Lord the church: For we are members of his body, of his flesh, and of his bones. For this cause shall a man leave his father and mother, and shall be joined unto his wife, and they two shall be one flesh. This is a great mystery: but I speak concerning Christ and the church. Nevertheless let every one of you in particular so love his wife even as himself; and the wife see that she reverence her husband.
  (Ephesians 5:21–33)

- **Marriage is good and honorable.**

  Marriage is honourable in all, and the bed undefiled: but whoremongers and adulterers God will judge. (Hebrews 13:4)

In conclusion, marriage is a beautiful relation instituted by God, solemnized by Jesus accepting an invitation to attend and participating in a wedding ceremony in Cana, as recorded in the gospel of John.

And the third day there was a marriage in Cana of Galilee; and the mother of Jesus was there: And both Jesus was called, and his disciples, to the marriage. And when they wanted wine, the mother of Jesus saith unto him, They have no wine. (John 2:1–3)

Jesus saith unto them, Fill the waterpots with water. And they filled them up to the brim. And he saith unto them, Draw out now, and bear unto the governor of the feast. And they bare it. (John 2:7–8)

It is true that many marriage relationships become distorted and fragmented and eventually end in divorce. Even though divorce is a reality, marriage is doable for life when biblical principles are entwined in the fabric of the marriage relationship.

Yes, it is true that many people do not entertain the idea of inviting God's principles into their marriage relationship. I contend that those marriages though good can be so much better if God's principles are applied.

Is your marriage good enough to get better? (Robert Cunningham)

Bibliography

Augsburger, David. *Caring Enough to Confront.* Ventura, Calif.: Regal Books, 1973.

Barnes, Bo. *Your Husband Your Friend.* Eugene, Oreg.: Harvest House Publishers, 1993.

Brill, Earl H. *Sex Is Dead.* New York: Seabury Press, 1967.

Carter, Les. *Grace and Divorce.* San Francisco: Jossey-Bass, 2005.

Chapman, Gary. *The Five Love Languages.* Chicago: Northfield Publishing, 1995.

Cooper Darien B. *We Became Wives of Happy Husbands.* Wheaton, Ill.: SP Publications, 1976.

Copelin, Mary Anne. *Fulfillment in Marriage.* Houston: Mary Anne Copelin (publisher), 1983.

Demarest, Gary. *Christian Alternatives within Marriage.* Waco, Tex.: Word Books, 1977.

Dycus, Barbara. *God's Design for Broken Lives.* Springfield, Mo.: Gospel Publishing House, 1994.

Eggerichs, Emerson. *Love and Respect*. Nashville: Thomas Nelson, 2004.

Feldhahn, Shaunti. *For Women Only*. Colorado Springs: Multnomah Publishers, 2004.

Feldhahn, Jeff, and Feldhahn, Shaunti. *For Men Only*. Colorado Springs: Multnomah Publishers, 2004.

Getz, Gene. *Building Up One Another*. Colorado Springs: NesxGen, 2005.

Glahn, Sandra, and Cutrer, William. *When Empty Arms Become a Heavy Burden*. Nashville: Broadman and Holman Publishers, 1997.

Hammond, Frank, and Hammond, Ida. *Pigs in the Parlor*. Kirkwood, Mo.: Impact Books, 1973.

Hammond, Michelle McKinney. *What to Do until Love Finds You*. Eugene, Oreg.: Harvest House, 1977.

Horner, Bob, and Horner, Jan. *Resolving Conflict in Your Marriage*. Ventura, Calif.: Gospel Light Publishing, 1993.

Jakes, T. D. *Loose That Man and Let Him Go*. Tulsa, Okla.: Albury Press, 1995.

Jenson, Mary. *Partners in Promise*. Sisters, Oreg.: Multnomah Books, 1996.

Karssen, Gien. *Her Name Is Woman*. Colorado Springs: The Navigators, 1975.

Kopp, Russell. *An Introduction to Family Systems*. Jacksonville, Fla.: Logos Christian College and Graduate School, 1992.

Kübler-Ross, Elisabeth. *On Death and Dying.* New York, Macmillan, 1969.

Lewis, Carol, and Symank, Cara. *The Mother Daughter Legacy.* Ventura, Calif.: Regal Books, 2004.

Lewis, Paul. *40 Ways to Teach Your Child Values.* Grand Rapids: Zondervan Publishing House, 1985.

Life Application Study Bible. Grand Rapids: Zondervan Publishing House, 2000.

Markman, Howard J.; Stanley, Scott; Blumberg, Susan L. *Fighting for Your Marriage.* San Francisco: Jossey-Bass, 2001.

McPherson, Miles. *The Power of Believing in Your Child.* Minneapolis: Bethany House Publishers, 1998.

Middlebrook, J. D., and Summers, Larry. *The Church and Family.* Springfield, Mo.: Gospel Publishing House, 1980.

Ogilvie, Lloyd John. *You Are Loved and Forgiven: Paul's Letter of Hope to the Colossians.* Ventura, Calif.: Regal Books, 1977.

Powell, John. *Why Am I Afraid to Tell You Who I Am?* Valencia, Calif.: Tabar Publishing, 1969.

Rainey, Dennis. *Ministering to Twenty-First Century Families.* Nashville: W Publishing Group, 2001.

Seamands, David A. *Healing for Damaged Emotions.* Colorado Springs: Life Journey Publishers, 2004.

Sherrer, Quin, and Garlock, Ruthanne. *A Spirit-Led Mom.* Eugene, Oreg.: Harvest House Publishers, 2004.

Smalley, Gary. *The DNA of Relationships*. Colorado Springs: Alive Communications, 2007.

Smalley, Gary, and Smalley, Greg. *Winning Your Husband Back Before It's Too Late*. Nashville: Thomas Nelson, 1999.

Rorie, Tony. *Raise Sons*. Dallas: Tony Rorie (publisher), 2006.

Rosenau, Douglas. *Slaying the Marriage Dragons*. Wheaton, Ill.: SP Publications, 1991.

Walker, James. *Husbands Who Won't Lead and Wives Who Won't Follow*. Minneapolis: Bethany House Publishers, 1989.

Wilson, Sandra D. *Hurt People Hurt People*. Grand Rapids: Discovery House Publishers, 1993.

Wright, Norman H. Moore. *Communication Keys for Your Marriage*. Ventura, Calif.: Regal Books, 1983.

HELP! I'M MARRIED!

A Note from the Author

Theodore and Nadine Hughes

I am convinced that a biblical relationship with God is necessary for a successful marriage. Everyone will need to talk to an outside party, either directly or indirectly, especially when the marriage relationship is shaky, sputtering, or stalled. These kinds of emotional challenges are a result of our human individuality and independence.

Even if a friend, counselor, or minister is called upon, he or she can advise only up to a point. When biblical principles are embraced, the advice given will go further and deeper because the Word of God never returns void and God will watch over His Word to assure its success. We should look at marriage difficulties not as closed doors but as a recipe for possibilities.

CPSIA information can be obtained
at www.ICGtesting.com
Printed in the USA
VHW021510150121
76576LV00011B/973